William Lloyd Garrison at Two Hundred

Since its founding in 1998, The Gilder Lehrman Center for the Study of Slavery, Resistance, and Abolition, which is part of the Yale Center for International and Area Studies, has sponsored an annual international conference on major aspects of the chattel slave system, its ultimate destruction, and its legacies in America and around the world. The Center's mission is, one, to increase knowledge of this story across time and all boundaries, and, two, to reach out to broader publics which demonstrate a growing desire to understand race, slavery, abolition, and the extended meanings of this history over time. Because the research, discoveries, and narratives presented at our conferences do so much to enrich our knowledge of one of humanity's most dehumanizing institutions and its place in the founding of the modern world, as well as of the first historical movements for human rights, we are immensely grateful to Yale University Press for engaging in this joint publication venture. The Gilder Lehrman Center is supported by Richard Gilder and Lewis Lehrman, generous Yale alumni and devoted patrons of American history. The Center aspires, with Yale University Press, to offer to the broadest possible audience the best modern scholarship on a story of global and lasting significance.

DAVID W. BLIGHT, Class of 1954 Professor of History at Yale University, and Director, Gilder Lehrman Center for the Study of Slavery, Resistance, and Abolition.

Edited by
J A M E S B R E W E R S T E W A R T

William Lloyd Garrison at Two Hundred

HISTORY, LEGACY, AND MEMORY

Yale University Pre

New Haven &

London

Set in Sabon Roman type by Keystone Typesetting, Inc.
Printed in the United States of America.

Library of Congress Cataloging-in-Publication Data

William Lloyd Garrison at two hundred : history, legacy, and memory / edited by James Brewer Stewart.
p. cm.
Includes bibliographical references and index.
ISBN-13: 978-0-300-13658-6 (alk. paper)
ISBN-10: 0-300-13658-7 (alk. paper)

1. Garrison, William Lloyd, 1805–1879. 2. Garrison, William Lloyd, 1805–1879 — Influence. 3. Garrison, William Lloyd, 1805–1879 — Political and social views. 4. Garrison, William Lloyd, 1805–1879 — Anniversaries, etc. 5. Abolitionists — United States — Biography. 6. Antislavery movements — United States — History — 19th century. I. Stewart, James Brewer. II. Garrison, William Lloyd, 1805–1879.
E449.G25W55 2008
326'.8092 — dc22
[B]   2008009403

This paper meets the requirements of ANSI/NISO Z39.48-1992 (Permanence of Paper).
It contains 30 percent postconsumer waste (PCW) and is certified by the Forest Stewardship Council (FSC).

10 9 8 7 6 5 4 3 2 1

Contents

Preface

Soon after his death in 1879, William Lloyd Garrison's children acted decisively in the hope that historians would never deny the central importance of their controversial father. Between 1885 and 1889 Wendell Phillips Garrison and Francis Jackson Garrison brought to publication four large volumes that chronicled their father's life much as he himself might have done it — that is, by presenting Garrison as the single most insightful, heroic, and, above all, significant leader in the abolitionists' thirty-year crusade to destroy slavery.

As it turned out, their timing could not have been worse.

In the same years that *William Lloyd Garrison, 1805–1879: The Story of His Life Told by His Children* came into print, the gains achieved by the struggle to which Garrison had dedicated his life — freedom and equal rights for African American people — were being brutally denied in the states of the old Confederacy and in much of the North as well. Lynching, exploitative sharecropping, inferior or nonexistent education, political disenfranchisement, and segregation spread rapidly across the South. Barriers against black equality likewise heightened enormously in the North as white Americans from both sides of the Mason-Dixon line set aside lingering grievances in favor of sectional "reunion" and deepening beliefs in white supremacy. In this post-Reconstruction era it was simple enough for almost everyone to agree that William Lloyd Garrison had stood foremost in the abolitionist cause, but that the cause itself had been insanely destructive and deeply misguided about black people's "innate capacities."

As the two hundredth anniversary of Garrison's birth drew closer, between 2001 and 2005 William Lloyd Garrison's great-great-grandchildren also acted on behalf of the historical memory of their ancestor. But instead of following Francis Jackson Garrison's and Wendell Phillips Garrison's example of collaborating on a biography, they organized a memorable bicentennial celebration. For three days in Boston in August 2005, Garrison family members (ultimately over 170 in all) hosted a major academic conference on and public celebration of the life of William Lloyd Garrison, sponsored by the Museum of African American History, the Boston Athenaeum, and the Boston Public Library. Several distinguished scholars made major presentations. Two, David W. Blight and Lois A. Brown, have revised their remarks for inclusion in this book. Substantial historical exhibits documented the abolitionists' struggles in Boston and major events in Garrison's life. Participants closely investigated historic sites on Boston's Freedom Trail. All the events, open to the general public, were heavily attended, particularly by members of greater Boston's black community.

The aim of the conference was not to magnify the reputation of a famous forbear, as Garrison's children had attempted. Instead, it sought answers to more searching questions about Garrison's significance in the nation's struggles for equality, both in his own lifetime and in more modern times. What were his qualities of leadership, both positive and negative? How can people today better understand what he believed in, what motivated him, how his impact might be assessed? What did his contemporaries see in him? What might his example mean to people today? How might memories of him have influenced those who succeeded him?

By asking such questions, these modern descendants intervened on William Lloyd Garrison's behalf in a way that could not have been more useful to historians or more pertinent to the present moment.

And the present moment is not encouraging. For well over a decade, the civil rights movement has continued to slip further into history, a process as replete with outcomes as disturbing as those that mocked the hopes of Garrison's children in the 1880s. In the current "post–civil rights" era, segregation and racial discrimination are everywhere illegal. On the one hand, a slowly expanding, if tenuously established, black middle class is developing. African American academicians and creative artists continue to challenge and enrich American culture, just as they always have. African Americans hold important positions at all levels of government and compete effectively for election to high office. Hosts of professional athletes and "megastar" entertainers incessantly project their images throughout the media. Black history month annually brings eloquent memorials to Dr. Martin Luther King Jr. and prideful claims about "how far our nation has come."

Yet simultaneously, as the ghastly impact of hurricane Katrina so vividly illuminated, a shockingly large number of urban African Americans are overborne by forces far beyond their control. They continue to face ever-increasing unemployment, impoverishment, isolation from the state and its social services, and victimization by both criminals and law enforcement. Overall, African Americans' expected life span declines in relation to that of whites, and infant mortality rates remain flat, even as statistics for whites continue to progress. Even with the advent of numerous superrich black professionals and celebrities, African Americans' aggregate net worth continues to lag relative to that of all other Americans. In response to these trends, neoconservative and neoliberal commentators alike, black and white together, condemn public assistance as "the new slavery," affirmative action as "undemocratic quotas," and African Americans' claims for justice as unwarranted "whining." Certain self-designated black leaders no longer represent broad African American constituencies but instead exploit racial tragedies in order to enhance their personal visibility. Racist ideologists posing as historians claim falsely that slavery played no role in causing the Civil War and that loyal slaves rallied in large numbers to fight for their Confederate masters.

So, in the midst of our age of resurgent racial oppression what, indeed, ought one to make of William Lloyd Garrison? How, at this current juncture, can the abolitionists' struggles on behalf of African American freedom and equality be properly understood? Drawing its inspiration directly from the Garrison family's bicentennial celebration of 2005, this book attempts to address precisely these questions.

David W. Blight's chapter, "William Lloyd Garrison at Two Hundred: His Radicalism and His Legacy for Our Time," provides a concise biographical portrait that raises important questions of memory and meaning. Blight asks, "Is the United States of the twenty-first century truly a safe place for William Lloyd Garrison and many of his ideas?" Answers become possible, Blight shows, once one comes to understand the early circumstances that led Garrison to become a charismatic religious visionary, the content and implications of his visions, and the reasons that they led him to such radical conclusions. Answers become clearer still, Blight suggests, once one possesses a fuller understanding of Garrison's disquieting position in the political culture of his age as well as of the powerful memories he evoked in those such as Frederick Douglass, who responded to him constantly over several decades.

Each of the four chapters that follow is concerned with evaluating a specific aspect of Garrison's leadership in the larger abolitionist crusade. The individual topics considered are, in order, internationalism, women's rights, state and local politics, and, finally, national politics. Each of the chapters also addresses comprehensively two other crucial issues, issues so basic to Garrison's ideology that they shaped his approach to every other cause he espoused: Christian nonresistance and African American liberation. This integrative approach, I believe, yields more contextualized understandings of these two most basic articles of the Garrisonian faith than would result from treating each separately in a stand-alone essay. This approach, moreover, offers the most direct way to assess for good or ill Garrison's leadership within the abolitionist movement as a whole.

Richard J. M. Blackett's " 'And There Shall Be No Sea': William Lloyd Garrison and the Transatlantic Abolitionist Movement" evaluates the three-decade quest by Garrison and his coworkers to stimulate among the British support for immediate emancipation. Their aim, as Blackett explains, was to "wall off and isolate America so that it would be left with no other option but to free its slaves." As Blackett considers the activities of Garrison and his many emissaries, it becomes clear that from the mid-1840s onward doctrines of religious perfectionism worked increasingly at cross-purposes in the creation of a truly effective Anglo-American abolitionist alliance. Too often, African American ambassadors such as Douglass and Charles Lenox Remond found themselves thrown off stride by white perfectionists who espoused such unpopular and seemingly unrelated causes as utopian socialism and nonresistance. Yet whatever its flaws, as Blackett observes, Garrison's lifelong campaign greatly expanded the horizons of American abolitionists, secured vital British support for the Union during the Civil War, and stimulated the internationalization of humanitarian concern.

Garrison's "broad application of abolitionist principles enabled him to play an integral part in the evolution of the feminist abolitionist movement," observes Lois A. Brown in her chapter entitled "William Lloyd Garrison and Emancipatory Feminism in Nineteenth-Century America." She proposes that emancipatory feminism had a significant impact on Garrison's politics and that he, in turn, influenced the ways in which women applied emancipatory feminism, women who were strictly abolitionists and women who strove to achieve gender equality, more broadly defined. The importance of these reciprocal influences becomes clear, Brown demonstrates, once Garrison's simultaneous demands for slave and female emancipation began stimulating extended and deeply contested explorations by abolitionist women of alternative roads to freedom for each of these marginalized groups. As such explorations went forward, Brown demonstrates, Garrison's words and actions decisively influenced the thoughts and choices of an extraordinary number of female activists, the unsung no less than the famous, black no less than white.

In his chapter "Putting Politics Back In: Rethinking the Problem of Political Abolitionism," Bruce Laurie offers a critical analysis of Garrison's political strategies and tactics in arenas in which their impact was felt most immediately, that is, within Massachusetts. Here, throughout the early and mid-1840s, Garrison and his allies pitted their nonvoting, perfectionist approaches to political issues of black equality against those of their hated abolitionist opponent, the Liberty Party, which fielded its own candidates, embraced electioneering, and formed coalitions with other influential parties. Laurie's findings present, at best, a mixed review of Garrison's political instincts and their consequences. When it came to issues vital to the interests of Massachusetts's black people, such as repealing laws that criminalized miscegenation and permitted segregation, Liberty men proved the more effective abolitionists. Though Garrisonians developed scathing moral condemnations of the party's practices, they also decried and encumbered the same legislative processes that the Liberty Party exploited for egalitarian ends. Moreover, when Liberty Party operatives attempted in the early 1840s to secure legal protections for fugitive slaves, Garrisonians' efforts on behalf of this same goal proved more hindrance than help. And finally, as Laurie notes, female abolitionists found in the Liberty Party opportunities to participate in genuine electoral politics that Garrison's antigovernment approaches could never offer them, which is, perhaps, why so many female abolitionists supported it.

James Brewer Stewart's "God, Garrison and the Coming of the Civil War" extends Laurie's concerns to the national level in asking the question, "What possible role could this ideologically marginal utopian have played in [the] . . . sectional division [that] drove the nation to Civil War?" Answers suggest themselves, Stewart contends, when one assesses the impact of the entire abolitionist movement, Garrisonians included, on the evolving sectional dynamics of the nation's two-party system. Throughout the 1840s even antipolitical abolitionists like Garrison exercised significant agency in national elections involving slavery issues that were contested by the Whigs and the Democrats. But as that agency eroded during the 1850s, Garrison stood at the forefront of an increasingly militant and violence-prone abolitionist movement that did much to deepen the atmosphere of impending North–South confrontation. At the same time, as Stewart emphasizes, the political agency exercised by the abolitionists was, though influential, always quite limited, a point illustrated by comparisons and contrasts between the abolitionist movement and right-wing evangelical politics today.

Lloyd McKim Garrison's "Garrison at Two Hundred: The Family, the Legacy, and the Question of Garrison's Relevance in Contemporary America" is the volume's coda. It reconsiders Blight's initial question: "Is the United States ... truly a safe place for William Lloyd Garrison and many of his ideas?" Lloyd McKim Garrison's detailing of the impressive commitments to egalitarian ideals lived out by so many of Garrison's direct descendants leaves the reader with the strong impression that the best answers arise from the legacies of the family's "founding father." As the chapter demonstrates, a vivid awareness of their extraordinary forbear continues to this day to define the family's collective memories and its individual members' pursuit of freedom and justice. While succeeding generations have updated family ideals when working to combat more modern forms of inequality, they have also extended unchanged the most vital elements of the original Garrison's spirit: his abhorrence of violence, his impatience with conventional wisdom, his rejection of complacency, and, above all, his insistence that people have a duty to bend the future in the direction of justice for all. America has never been safe for Garrison's beliefs, and it is indisputably not safe now. Yet this, of course, is precisely the reason his history remains so challenging and his legacies so deeply in conflict with the nation Americans are fashioning in the twenty-first century.

William Lloyd Garrison at Two Hundred

William Lloyd Garrison at Two Hundred:
His Radicalism and His Legacy for Our Time

DAVID W. BLIGHT

What is man born for but to be a Reformer, a Re-maker of what man has made; a renouncer of lies; a restorer of truth and good, imitating that great Nature which embosoms us all, and which sleeps no moment on an old past, but every hour repairs herself, yielding us every morning a new day, and with every pulsation a new life? Let him renounce everything which is not true to him, and put all his practices back on their first thoughts, and do nothing for which he has not the whole world for his reason. — *Ralph Waldo Emerson, "Man the Reformer,"* 1841

William Lloyd Garrison is a storied, troubling, challenging, profoundly important, and controversial historical figure. Along with Frederick Douglass, there was no more significant American reformer in the nineteenth century. It was not always safe to be William Lloyd Garrison, in his hometown of Boston or anywhere in the United States. He was deeply loved and respected by his family and closest friends and followers. For many good reasons he was called Father Garrison by the beloved, turbulent, quarrelsome band known as the Garrisonians. And at home he was a fun-loving, kind husband and father who delighted in the household that Helen Benson Garrison, his wife, crafted for him. But in most of America he was vilified, hated, denounced — so much so that he was once nearly lynched as the most dangerous newspaper editor in the land, a role he often relished.

Is the United States of the early twenty-first century truly a safe place for William Lloyd Garrison and many of his ideas? In this age when North and South and proslavery and antislavery have been replaced by a new "house divided," riven this time by region (red and blue states) and by religion (those who would obliterate and those who would preserve the lines between church and state), how should people today remember Garrison?[1] In a society divided by social and cultural issues of privacy and sexuality, between those who believe in government as an agent of human betterment and social change and those who do not believe in government at all, preferring a world driven by an unbridled global market, and in the midst of yet another foreign war of dubious origins and aims, where is the place for this great radical in modern debates? How does Garrison speak to people today? What kind of a model is he in a time when the term *abolitionist* is appropriated freely by people across the political spectrum — those concerned to eradicate the new forms of slavery and human exploitation emerging in the world, and those who seek to abolish a woman's right to reproductive freedom, or the Endangered Species Act, or Social Security, or redistributive justice, or National Public Radio, or the estate tax? Who or what is an abolitionist today?

Only a few days after Garrison's funeral in late May 1879, Douglass delivered an extraordinary eulogy in Philadelphia to his fallen comrade, with whom he had shared a deep, pivotal friendship but also a long, bitter estrangement. Death had been thinning the ranks of the old abolitionists year after year, and Douglass solemnly lamented that those who remained "may be found standing like stately pillars of a fallen temple as belonging to another age." Douglass worried that the story of abolitionism was becoming the history beyond memory. It was a "thrilling story," said Douglass. "But soon . . . no living witness will be left to tell it." Such is the fate of all historical movements, leaders, great ideas, turning points. The holders of a flame, the authors of an idea, the leaders of a revolution always worry about the transience of their work. Douglass felt some confidence that the abolitionist saga would survive because it was an ascendant story, from "weakness to strength, from conflict to victory, and from shame to glory." How American, he seemed to suggest. And as though remembering Garrison's very own thoughts, the former slave claimed that the movement's significance might endure because it could be seen in "the fire and fury with which it was assailed in its infancy, how the Herods of that day sought its infant life, how its friends were sometimes only rescued from danger and death by hiding themselves from the wrath and fury of the mob."[2]

But Douglass had good reason to worry. Once a great historical change like emancipation, the modern civil rights revolution, the New Deal regulatory state, or a transformative war enters the realm of historical interpretation and collective memory formation, those who can control the narrative of the past are likely to control the meaning of those changes in the present and future. It seems a truism, but how often we have to be reminded that the struggle over historical memory is always a battle in which versions of the past are used as instruments of power. Today, it would seem that Americans are virtually all abolitionists. Douglass and Harriet Tubman are obligatory pictures in every textbook and classroom, and what town from Tennessee northward does not seem to need its site or "depot" on the Underground Railroad in heritage tourism, one of the fastest growing businesses in America? Unless one remains skeptical, Underground Railroad enthusiasm may give virtually every American the right to think that we all freed the slaves.[3] And it is both wonderful and sometimes disturbing to see how in schooling and textbooks, abolitionists have moved over into the good ledger of America's heroes, rather than being portrayed as the tiny minority of dangerous, vilified, hated rebels they were deemed to be in their own time. We should beware, as Saleem, the protagonist in Salman Rushdie's novel *Midnight's Children,* warns: "Memory [is] truth," he says, "because memory has its own special kind. It selects, eliminates, alters, exaggerates, minimizes, glorifies, and vilifies also; but in the end it creates its own reality."[4]

Douglass had good reason to worry in the wake of Reconstruction, as the original Republican Party retreated from its principles, the white South took back control of its race relations, and white supremacy thrived in a climate of resentment, hatred, and violence. As the former Confederate South began to fashion its own new victory narrative — its triumph over Reconstruction — out of its Lost Cause culture, the emancipationist memory of the Civil War would increasingly find itself on the defensive. Douglass knew this full well as he eulogized his former abolitionist mentor in 1879. "Our country is again in trouble," he announced. "The ship of state is again at sea . . . she trembles and plunges . . . every timber in her vast hull is made to feel the heavy strain." These were Garrisonian metaphors, pulled from the recesses of the magnificent moral imagination these two giants had shared. "A spirit of evil has been revived," Douglass warned, and "doctrines are proclaimed . . . which were, as we thought, all extinguished by the iron logic of cannonballs." Just who and what had won the Civil War was not yet settled, Douglass maintained on this sad day, and in what he called "this second battle for liberty and nation," he declared he would "sorely miss the mind and voice of William Lloyd Garrison."[5]

Garrison was the young man who all but raised himself from true poverty and neglect and who grew up determined never to become Abijah Garrison, his drunken-sailor father who abandoned his family when William was three, or his older brother, James, a desperate alcoholic who also went to sea to fail. William became a young printer's apprentice driven by at least two impulses: one, to change the world through a moral revolution in the attitudes and practices, even the character, of humankind; and two, a deep personal ambition to be the man who would lead that moral revolution and gain world recognition for his heroic, even martyred effort.[6]

Garrison's early biography is a stunning American story of achievement against all odds. From age seven on, young Garrison lived a rootless, impoverished existence, shunted to friends who cared for him while his mother, Fanny Garrison, moved from town to town in search of better employment as a domestic servant. He lived apart from his mother for at least seven years. To understand him, a good place to start is his mother's consuming Baptist piety. She inspired in her son a deep sense of Christian guilt and conscience, of the saving power of Jesus, and of one's obligation to testify in some way to one's own spiritual rebirth. The adult Garrison's abiding, formidable seriousness as a Christian moralist has its roots in his mother's strictures to walk only in God's sanctified paths. He was largely self-educated and, after attaining fame above all else for his wielding of words, he claimed he "did not understand one rule of grammar."[7] At the age of thirteen he entered a seven-year apprenticeship as a printer, and it was from voracious reading, but also from his employment as a typesetter (a task he loved), that he came to hear the music of language in his head. Words were his weapon against his harsh world even as a teenager, when he began to write his first editorials excoriating corrupt politicians. This spiritually driven youth would not enter the clergy; he wanted a more public platform from which to thrash the immorality of the world, and he found his calling as a journalist. He would leave a mark on American history like few others as a testament to the power of a free press and of the freedom of expression.[8]

Such a public role, though, deeply worried his mother. In letters they exchanged, young William Lloyd desperately sought his mother's approval but did not always get it. She worried that, like all writers, he would "starve to death in some garret or place that no one inhabits." She begged her son not to join "them class of people." And even if he succeeded, if he wrote about the nasty world of politics, she admonished, he would be corrupted and lose his "soul."[9] But as Garrison entered the public arena, he did so as a believer in fixed principles, as a thoroughgoing moralist who rejected all forms of compromise.

Yet Fanny's warnings would constitute the core of Garrison's personal dilemma: how to square sanctification with worldly success, his own moral purity with fame and ambition. And he was immensely ambitious — both to save the world and to emancipate himself from his sordid past, from that memory itself of a childhood lived in the face of his father's and brother's perdition and of begging for scraps of leftover food at the back door of rich people's homes. Early on, Garrison became very political in the ways he disdained and attacked the craft of politics. And he was determined to make a sinful world notice him. This was a young man, after all, who commissioned his own portrait at age nineteen, and at twenty-one bought his own newspaper, the Newburyport *Herald,* on a loan from Ephraim Allen, the master he served as an apprentice.[10] Garrison did not come to the table of abolitionism with noblesse oblige, honed in refinement and education; he came hungry and angry and in need of his own liberation as he learned about the desperation of millions that had been caused by slavery in America.

Fanny Garrison went lonely and broken to her grave in 1823 as her son grew into a young radical in the environment of the religious revivals and evangelical reform fervor of the 1820s. Like so many of the new generation of abolitionists about to launch what would become the greatest reform movement in American history, Garrison was inspired by the preachings of Lyman Beecher, Charles Grandison Finney, and others. He learned his denunciatory and combative style and the craft of moral suasion, the idea that the hearts of men and women must be changed before any laws or political structures can change, in an environment of great geographic expansion, social upheaval, and the increasingly radical reform of the 1820s.

Between 1827 and 1830, in Boston, Burlington, Vermont, and Baltimore, Maryland, Garrison edited and wrote for three more papers, all of which would fail on his watch. When he met Benjamin Lundy, the editor of the *Genius of Universal Emancipation* (in Baltimore), he came under the influence of a genuinely radical abolitionist. It was here that Garrison converted to immediatism, the argument that slaves had the inherent right to their freedom instantly and that all efforts should be exercised, peacefully, to make that happen. But immediatism was also a method, a disposition, almost a religion unto itself. It meant that any delay in the liberation of humans held as the property of other humans was intolerable. Garrison honed his moral suasion now as though he were sounding fire alarms against all manner of iniquity. He seems to have loved his role, as the historian James B. Stewart puts it, as "uncompromising moral censor." And he would measure "his value by the fury of his opponents." His style became so harsh that one critic compared him to the "pert loquacity of a blue-jay," and he was condemned north and south as a dangerous threat to the social and economic order. Moreover, a slave trader in Baltimore whom Garrison attacked sued him for libel. Convicted and unable to pay the one-hundred-dollar fine, the twenty-four-year-old editor was jailed for nearly fifty days. His imprisonment became a badge of honor, a drama of martyrdom he likened to that of the apostle Paul. "So agreeable is my confinement," he wrote, that his adversity was "like oil to the flame of my zeal. I am not dismayed, but bolder and more confident than ever. . . . I will not hold my peace on the subject of African oppression. If need be who would not die a martyr to such a cause?"[11] The wealthy Tappan brothers, Lewis and Arthur, of New York bailed Garrison out of jail, helped him return to Boston, and raised money to support a new paper that would truly last.

On January 1, 1831, Garrison published the first issue of the *Liberator,* which was published from 1831 to 1865 and became the longest-lasting antislavery publication in America. In that paper, month after month, he threw down the gauntlet and breathed fire into a crusade in search of leadership. Through the *Liberator* and through the Massachusetts and eventually the American Antislavery Society, Garrison forged a series of principles and doctrines over the next decade and a half that increasingly raised the bar of moral purity and the standards of abolitionist philosophy and practice. Those principles are roughly the following:

1. Moral perfectionism: a stern, demanding call for abolitionists to remove themselves as much as possible from the corrupting influences of secular and religious institutions, to seek personal holiness and follow the biblical injunction "Be ye perfect, even as your heavenly Father is perfect."

2. Nonresistance and pacifism: Taking literally the biblical injunction "Be ye perfect as your Father in heaven is perfect," Garrison rejected all acts of violence, even in self-defense, and advocated allegiance only to a government of God. All "coercive" institutions and laws were restraints on individual freedom of conscience; he urged his followers to "come-out" from hypocritical and morally polluted organizations such as political parties, legislatures, and even formal churches.

3. Anticlericalism: Garrison became deeply alienated from and a fierce critic of formal religion, especially the Protestant clergy, whom he saw as complicitous with slavery, intemperance, and all manner of moral imperfection in society. Some of his strongest venom was expended on those he perceived as remote, corrupt ministers, whom he called, among other epithets, "disgraces to humanity . . . heathenish . . . accessories to the man-stealers."

4. Disunionism: Garrison advocated northern withdrawal from the American Union as a way of ceasing to cooperate in evil. He argued that the U. S. Constitution was explicitly proslavery in several provisions, "a covenant with death, and an agreement with hell." For much of its life, the *Liberator*'s masthead carried the slogan, "No Union with the Slaveholders!"

Only if all Christians took this radical stand, Garrisonians believed, could the nation come to its senses and rise to a collective moral revolution that would end slavery by acts of will rather than by force.

5. Boycotting elections: As political abolitionism took hold in the 1840s, Garrison actively opposed voting as a hollow ritual, an act that sustained the godless compromising of American politics in regard to slavery. The true citizen kept his own soul pure first and by his moral witness would draw the rest of society along with him. During this period of his career, Garrison essentially saw politics itself as hopelessly immoral by definition.

6. Women's rights and equality: Early on, Garrison supported the civil and political rights of women as well as their right to free expression. His feminism extended to welcoming women into positions of authority in antislavery societies, although not to support of a women's sexual revolution. Few issues divided abolitionists and caused their famous schism in 1840 quite like the role of women in their movement.

7. African American civil rights: Garrison welcomed blacks to his home as guests and to his printing office as assistants, and he led campaigns to end segregation on railroads and in the Boston public schools. He demanded all civil rights for blacks, and they made up the great majority of subscribers to his newspaper. In his racial views and actions, Garrison was far ahead of almost all white northerners. Many black abolitionists, especially in New England, gave great allegiance to Garrison, whose commitment, courage, and uncompromising immediatism they trusted and found in no other white leader. When traveling with his black associates, Garrison always rode in the Blacks Only railway car.[12]

Garrison maintained that he never really made these principles into tests of membership in the American Antislavery Society; he always said others were free to dissent. He could, however, be intolerant and dogmatic in his close circle of Garrisonian adherents. Garrison's claims to the contrary, Douglass most emphatically disagreed that Garrison had not made his fixed principles into standards of allegiance, even of friendship. Garrison needed, sometimes demanded, loyalty to his leadership and his method.[13]

As abstract ideals, nonresistance, nonvoting, and disunionism tore apart the antislavery movement. For blacks especially, many of whom were former slaves who wore the scars of this bondage on their backs and in their psyches, the emergencies of freedom, security, and basic rights did not permit them the luxury of debate over the ideological or strategic purity that sometimes occupied white abolitionists. Garrison would himself eventually adopt a strain of such pragmatism — in the Civil War, when events overwhelmed his perfectionism. Indeed, once the war became a crusade for human freedom and not merely an effort to preserve a status quo antebellum, the Union war effort had few stronger supporters than this former staunch pacifist. For their part, black abolitionists had anticipated the great philosopher of pragmatism William James. The theory of pragmatism, always keeping an open mind and testing one's truths, wrote James, "has no objection whatever to the realizing of abstractions, so long as you get about among particulars with their aid and they actually carry you somewhere."[14]

Anyone who set creeds like the ones described above as their standard for life and reform strategy would forever walk in a minefield of contradiction and paradox. As one of his own flock said, it was very difficult to "swallow Garrison whole."[15] Garrison desperately clung to his pacifism until John Brown's raid in 1859 and the coming of the Civil War broke its back in 1861. And in the early 1850s he had cheered many a fugitive slave rescue carried out at gunpoint, while maintaining that for him at least, violence was still a sin. His disunionism and philosophy of nonvoting shattered the antislavery movement like no other doctrines as many abolitionists saw the wisdom of political action in a nation dividing so openly over the expansion of slavery into the West. Garrison loathed the Liberty and Free Soil parties in the 1840s (he saw early antislavery politics as nothing but moral compromise), yet by the late 1850s, he wished to take credit for the evolution of an antislavery coalition like the Republican Party, with its capacity to threaten the South and its peculiar institution. As moral suasion itself teetered on bankruptcy or irrelevancy in the crisis-ridden 1850s, especially among blacks, Garrison labored as an astute observer of the elections he would not embrace, as a political junky who tried to maintain his moral opposition to the dirty world of politics. And during the Civil War, Garrison joined the Union cause wholeheartedly, warmly supported Abraham Lincoln (more strongly than Wendell Phillips and other abolitionists), especially after the Emancipation Proclamation, and fought tooth and nail all over again with some of his closest friends about whether black, male voting rights ought to follow freedom. He was lukewarm at best on black suffrage.

But as Ralph Waldo Emerson said so nicely, "A foolish consistency is the hobgoblin of little minds. . . . With consistency a great soul has simply nothing to do. . . . Speak what you think now in hard words and tomorrow speak what tomorrow thinks in hard words again."[16] Garrison would have been hard-pressed to admit that he followed this advice over time. He never seems to have believed that he really abandoned his perfectionism; his high ideals in search of the moral revolution, he believed, came about in the "jubilee" of the Civil War. Events vindicated his ideology, he contended. And he would strongly dispute the notion that it was the Union armies and the self-willed bravery of blacks themselves that freed the slaves, rather than the abolitionists. He was fully willing to accept responsibility for the abolitionists' role in bringing on the war. As a prophet who, by his understanding, came to witness his prophecy, Garrison needed to live in a victory narrative, creeds still intact, the moral foundation unshaken, the principles still fixed. Self-deception can stymie the soul, but it can also be a powerful prod to growth and change.

During his heyday as the spiritual and intellectual force behind radical abolitionism (1830s–40s), however, Garrison left an eternal imprint on the nature of radicalism in America. He was the genuine article — a radical perfectionist who demanded vast social changes that Americans were almost wholly unprepared and unwilling to accept. He threw thunderbolts at anyone and everyone he deemed responsible for slavery, the "crime of crimes" and "sin of sins" as he called it.[17] In language alone he left a legacy like few others. Garrison named his own lesson and his model when it came to answering for why he was so vitriolic in his denunciations of people and institutions: "If you would make progress, you must create opposition; if you would promote peace on earth, array the father against the son, the mother against the daughter; if you would save your reputation, lose it. It is a gospel paradox, but nevertheless true — the more peaceable a man becomes, after the pattern of Christ, the more he is inclined to make a disturbance, to be aggressive, to 'turn the world upside down.' "[18] If Jesus was indeed his model, it was the angry, revolutionary Jesus he most admired. His was the Jesus who could never be a joiner, only the leader. He would bear the cross, but he marched on with it, waving it at evil in the world as he found it. "Did Jesus of Nazareth," he was fond of asking, "care how many votes he got?"[19]

Garrison relished the status of despised minority in a righteous cause. He welcomed the hatred, even the violence, of his enemies. If he offended his readers, it was not his fault. "If I have exceeded the bounds of moderation," he wrote as early as 1831, "the monstrous turpitude of the times has transported me." Lest one think he saw himself as a selfless reformer only, he freely admitted that if people were offended by his "unequivocal language . . . so shall reformation advance, and my own soul obtain perfect satisfaction." And when he was nearly killed by a mob in Boston in 1835 and put in jail for safekeeping, he faced his adversaries, apparently, with great courage and even joy. That nine-foot gallows erected in front of his house in Roxbury by another mob no doubt unnerved him and his family. Physical attacks, though, were vindicating and sanctifying to the cause, he seemed to believe. "Give me brickbats in the cause of God," he wrote, "to wedges of gold in the cause of sin."[20]

If there is any secret to understanding Garrison's radicalism (in the 1830s–40s) it may be embodied in an old and often discredited idea: perfectionist *anarchism*. Today people think of an anarchist as a bomb-throwing terrorist or as the wildly dressed fringe elements at an antiglobalization protest. One looks at them with contemptuous if curious amusement, as practitioners of a disdainful absurdity in a world of so much chaos, fear, and violence. But the term can be used seriously and in historical context in reference to Garrison and his followers.

First of all, no one called himself an anarchist in antebellum America; as a term, it gained currency in Europe and the United States only in the late nineteenth century. To grasp Garrison's brand of anarchism, one must see it not as the advocacy of disorder, an absence of government itself. Garrison was the kind of idealist who sought to replace human governments and institutions with a "government of God," ruled by kinds of laws higher than legislatures, in their inherently compromising ways, can create. Garrison sought a new order, not the absence of order; he saw slavery as so evil because it denied human beings moral agency, the control over their own mind and body. In a society so infused with slavery, with its raw materials, its wealth, its legal foundations, its racism, its assumptions of invulnerability, Garrison concluded, abolitionism had to offer an alternative government, one in which humans did not put themselves above God. The true anarchists, to Garrison, the real destroyers of social order, were the slaveholders and all their apologists. "Non-resistance makes men self-governed," he said in 1855. "The kingdom of God is within them. Some speak of anarchy in connection with non-resistance. But this principle teaches those who receive it to be just, and upright, and kind, and true, in all the relations of life. It is the men of violence who furnish anarchists."[21] With this holy, utopian standard of human conduct, Garrison laid down his challenge: perfect thyself; do not return evil for evil; make all humankind your country; take responsibility for the nation's sins, past and present, and thereby free thyself by freeing the slave.

In his eulogy of 1879, Douglass remembered hearing Garrison speak for the first time forty years earlier in New Bedford, Massachusetts. Douglass was twenty-one years old and less than a year out of slavery. And what a memory he drew upon. Garrison, Douglass thought, "complied with Emerson's idea of a true reformer. It was not the utterance, but the man behind it that gave dignity, weight and effect to his speech." He went to the speech, he remarked, to see the "chief apostle" of abolitionism. The meeting was in "old Liberty Hall . . . a large, but dilapidated old place. Its woodwork was marred and defaced, its doors off hinges, and its windows broken by stones and other missiles thrown to break up abolition meetings." Through these mystic memories, Douglass gazed back to Garrison's image and his importance. "What a countenance was there!" he rhapsodized. "What firmness and benignity, what evenness of temper, what serenity of mind, what sweetness of spirit, what sublime intelligence were written as by the pen of an angel on that countenance!" A year escaped from slavery, the young, dislocated but excited fugitive must have felt transported that day. "In him," remembered Douglass, "I saw the resurrection and the life of the dead and buried hope of my long enslaved people." Garrison was not an orator of great gestures and rhetorical flourishes; his power rested not so much in affect or style as in the seriousness of his argument and his commitment. "His one single purpose," concluded Douglass with Garrisonian firmness, "was to excite sympathy for the enslaved, and make converts to the doctrine that slavery was a sin against God and man, and ought to be immediately abolished."[22] The doctrinal disputes and personal conflicts between Douglass and Garrison were well into the future from the day that memory took root in the young man's mind. Douglass found Garrison irresistible as an inspiration, as a source of hope in the face of overwhelming odds and of the power of racist and slaveholding America, at the same time he found him impossible to follow as a perfectionist visionary. He forever honored and admired the prophet, even if he could not remain in his church.

Garrison was an all-too-human utopian. But he was not the utopian who stayed outside of history, quietly sustained on faith and wish fulfillment alone. He ultimately joined the history of his time, helped make it, took credit for it, and, as a self-proclaimed prophet, inspired others to make a choice to either follow him or condemn him. However unreachable his standards were for poor, human frailty, one ignores the Garrisons of history at one's peril. Utopians are bothersome people: they trouble the water, they break the rules, disturb the peace, and irk the citizenry out of complacency, forcing unwanted confrontations with the eternal conflict between the possible and the ideal. What, after all, is life for but to find answers to that paradox of knowing just how to distinguish what *is* from what ought to be?

Notes

1. In June 1858 Abraham Lincoln famously used the biblical injunction that "a house divided against itself cannot stand," but Garrison had made frequent use of the metaphor before that. For example, at a meeting in New York of the American Antislavery Society in May 1855, three years before Lincoln's speech, Garrison intoned, "A church or government which accords the same rights and privileges to Slavery as to Liberty, is a house divided against itself, and cannot stand." For quote, see William E. Cain, ed., *William Lloyd Garrison and the Fight Against Slavery: Selections from the Liberator* (Boston: Bedford Books, 1995), 20.

2. Frederick Douglass, "Speech on the Death of William Lloyd Garrison," at Garrison memorial meeting, June 2, 1879, Fifteenth Street Presbyterian Church, Philadelphia, in Frederick Douglass Papers, Library of Congress, reel 15.

3. See David W. Blight, ed., *Passages to Freedom: The Underground Railroad in History and Memory* (Washington, D.C.: Smithsonian Books, 2004).

4. Salman Rushdie, *Midnight's Children* (New York: Penguin Books, 2000), 37.

5. Douglass, "Speech on the Death of William Lloyd Garrison."

6. For this insight of Garrison's two conflicting impulses, see James Brewer Stewart, *William Lloyd Garrison and the Challenge of Emancipation* (Arlington Heights, Ill.: Harlan Davidson, 1992), 19–25.

7. Quoted in ibid., 18; for the importance of Fanny Garrison's piety, see ibid., 2–11.

8. For Garrison's early biography in rich, narrative detail, see Henry Mayer, *All on Fire: William Lloyd Garrison and the Abolition of Slavery* (New York: St. Martins, 1998), 3–188.

9. Quotes in Stewart, *William Lloyd Garrison*, 21.

10. Ibid., 24.

11. Quotes in ibid., 46–47. On the influence of Lundy and on immediatism, see Mayer, *All on Fire*, 55–60, 70–94. For understanding immediatism I have also relied on Aileen Kraditor, *Means and Ends in American Abolitionism: Garrison and His Critics on Strategy and Tactics, 1834–1850* (New York: Vintage, 1967), chap. 2.

12. For the character of these Garrisonian principles, I have relied on Stewart, *William Lloyd Garrison*; Mayer, *All on Fire*; Cain, ed., *William Lloyd Garrison and the Fight Against Slavery*; Kraditor, *Means and Ends in American Abolitionism*; and especially Walter M. Merrill and Louis Ruchames, eds., *The Letters of William Lloyd Garrison*, 6 vols. (Cambridge: Harvard University Press, 1971–81); and Lewis Perry, *Radical Abolitionism: Anarchy and the Government of God in Antislavery Thought* (Ithaca: Cornell University Press, 1973).

13. On Douglass's break with Garrison, see David W. Blight, *Frederick Douglass' Civil War: Keeping Faith in Jubilee* (Baton Rouge: Louisiana State University Press, 1989) 26–31; and Mayer, *All on Fire*, 371–74, 431–33.

14. William James, "What Pragmatism Means" (1907), in *Pragmatism*, ed. Bruce Kuklick, 35–36 (Indianapolis: Hackett Publishing, 1981).

15. Quoted in Stewart, *William Lloyd Garrison*, 104.

16. Ralph Waldo Emerson, "Self-Reliance," in *Selected Essays: Ralph Waldo Emerson*, ed. Larzer Ziff, 183 (New York: Penguin, 1982).

17. Quoted in Mayer, *All on Fire*, 583.

18. *Liberator*, November 23, 1838.

19. Quoted in Stewart, *William Lloyd Garrison*, 126; and on Garrison's modeling of Jesus, see Cain, ed., *William Lloyd Garrison and the Fight Against Slavery*, 38.

20. Quotes in Cain, ed., *William Lloyd Garrison and the Fight Against Slavery*, 38; and Stewart, *William Lloyd Garrison*, 88.

21. Quote in Perry, *Radical Abolitionism*, 53.

22. Douglass, "Speech on the Death of William Lloyd Garrison."

2

"And There Shall Be No More Sea": William Lloyd Garrison and the Transatlantic Abolitionist Movement

RICHARD J. M. BLACKETT

When in early 1865 the Stars and Stripes were once again raised over Fort Sumter, William Lloyd Garrison and George Thompson, the British abolitionist, were there to witness the symbolic reuniting of the country at the end of a brutal civil war. It seemed a fitting culmination to the work of the two men who together had struggled for over thirty years to keep the transatlantic abolitionist movement together and who were considered by their peers to be the two pivotal figures in the struggle to win freedom for slaves in the United States. Inspired in part by Garrison's bold internationalist declaration, "Our Country is the World—Our Countrymen Are Mankind," they had between them crisscrossed the Atlantic half a dozen times in a quest to rally public opinion in favor of abolition. Their efforts did not always pay immediate dividends, but, standing at the site where the first shots in the war were fired, both men could take some comfort in the fact that their persistence and commitment to the cause of emancipation had finally borne fruit. The movement had wobbled at times and on occasion even cracked, but the frequent exchange of visits they and others made had managed to maintain a semblance of unity in an otherwise fractious alliance. The exchanges of letters, books, and pamphlets were crucial means of contact, but what held the movement together was the exchange of visits during which friendships were forged and renewed, money raised, and attempts made to influence public opinion in favor of emancipation.

The international contacts were particularly important to the movement in the United States in the years following West Indian emancipation in 1834. The success of British abolitionists set a standard to which all Americans, eager to see the abolition of slavery at home, could aspire. For the next thirty years American abolitionists made frequent tours of Britain, convinced, as Frederick Douglass said, that British public support could wall off and so isolate America that it would be left no other option but to free its slaves. The forging of this transatlantic alliance, however, proved more difficult than anyone could have anticipated. National jealousies were ever present and at times affected the alliance's ability to function. Down through the antebellum years supporters of slavery made every effort to exploit these tensions by raising the specter of British interference in American domestic affairs. When Thompson made his first trip to the United States a year after West Indian emancipation he was hailed as a foreign incendiary and greeted by violent mobs pledged to expel him if not take his life. Harriet Beecher Stowe was ridiculed for consorting with effete aristocracies during her tour of Britain in the 1850s. In spite of the abolitionists' best efforts there were times when the alliance stumbled over these national jealousies. That they kept their feet and continued to promote the cause, however, says a great deal about the movement's resilience. Understanding these tensions and difficulties is vital to an appreciation of the movement's accomplishments.

The fact that it took a bloody civil war to finally bring about emancipation does not in any way diminish the significance of the transatlantic movement, which had its beginnings in the months leading up to West Indian emancipation and the effort of American colonizationists to win British support for their plans to settle free blacks and freed slaves in Liberia. Established in 1816, the American Colonization Society (ACS) had by 1830 become a major force in the debate over emancipation. Its solution was simple. Given the level of prejudice against blacks in America, it was in the interest of all concerned to find a home for African Americans away from the United States. In the decade since the establishment of Liberia the ACS had attracted support from both those who saw it as a means to ensure emancipation and those who were convinced that the removal of the "disruptive" free black population would guarantee the continuation of slavery. By 1830 the inevitable tension created by these conflicting objectives had resulted in the departure of many members of the society, such as Garrison, who questioned the degree to which the society was committed to emancipation. Those who left threw in their lot with African Americans, who, by and large, had been opposed to the society from its inception, viewing it as nothing more than a poorly disguised apologist for slavery. Confronted by continued black opposition to its plans and the loss of members to the abolitionist movement, the society found itself in dire financial straits by 1830. In an effort to address these problems the society sent the Philadelphia Quaker Elliot Cresson on a tour of Britain.

Cresson's visit to Britain and his initial success in winning support for the society's efforts in Liberia set the stage for the emergence of the transatlantic movement. By diverting attention away from the principle of equality colonizationists insisted, as Aileen Kraditor has argued, that "Negro inferiority rather than white racism" was the source of the problem. This is why abolitionists of every stripe, black and white, were able to ignore other differences and rally against the ACS so effectively and why its plans became the first issue to garner the attention of the movement on both the national and international scene.[1] Soon after his arrival Cresson held a series of private meetings throughout the country in which he emphasized the antislavery thrust of the ACS and Liberia's potential to impede the slave trade and introduce Christianity to West Africa. In a public circular Cresson declared, "The great objects of the Society were the final and entire abolition of slavery providing for the best interest of the blacks, by establishing them in independence upon the coast of Africa, thus constituting them the protectors of the unfortunate natives against the inhuman ravages of the slaver seeking, through them, to spread the lights of civilization and Christianity among fifty millions who inhabited the dark regions."[2] This appeal to what can be called the "civilizationist principle," long part and parcel of British antislavery efforts in both the West Indies and Africa, was guaranteed to win Cresson support. Victorians assumed that Africans, like all backward peoples, were woefully lacking in civilization, something that had to be acquired if they were to avoid extinction. It was the responsibility of caring people to lend a helping hand to lift them out of barbarism. Cresson's appeal resonated with those who had long held to the principle that legitimate trade and the guiding hand of Christianity, carried, in this case, by the descendants of those who had suffered most from slavery but in the process had been exposed to Christianity, would ensure both the spread of civilization in Africa and the freedom of slaves in the United States. Many were impressed by Cresson's portrayal of the society's efforts. William Wilberforce and Thomas Clarkson, the grand old men of British abolitionism, publicly endorsed the society, as did Thompson, who wrote his wife that Cresson had shown "a spirit of the purest friendship," a view he would later come to regret.[3]

But Cresson did not have things all his own way. James Cropper, the Liverpool merchant, rejected Cresson's claims for the society. And Captain Charles Stuart, the eccentric Englishman who had lived and worked in Canada and the United States in the 1820s, published a series of anticolonization pamphlets and dogged Cresson wherever he went, challenging him to public debates about the society and its work. Stuart's indictment chastised the ACS for insisting there could be no emancipation without emigration; for acknowledging the slaveholders' right to continue holding slaves; for rejecting the notion of the unity of the races, a rejection which violated Christian teachings of the unity of man; and for ignoring the impossibility of removing the black population "without even the pretence of a crime against them, to a foreign and barbarous land," an act of "criminal absurdity." Let us, he warned, "cede to the American Colonization Society the principle that the negroes of the United States must not be emancipated in their native country, and that whether enslaved or free, they must be *transported,* and we cede our principle."[4]

No one interested in promoting antislavery, Stuart believed, should support an organization which substituted "banishment for slavery." Nor should they support a policy that was almost universally despised by those it was supposed to benefit. Instead, if they were genuinely interested in supporting a settlement which provided a refuge for the oppressed, then they should look to Wilberforce, a recently established black colony in what was then Upper Canada. The colony had been founded by African Americans who had fled Cincinnati, Ohio, following a series of attacks on their community in 1829. In early 1832, the fledgling colony sent the Reverend Nathaniel Paul, a Baptist minister from Albany, New York, on a fund-raising tour of Britain. Paul promptly joined forces with Stuart. Because he was a representative of the black-led colony his opposition to the ACS lent legitimacy to the campaign against Cresson. If African Americans, the potential beneficiaries of the society's plans, were adamantly opposed to its emigrationist scheme, then men of good will had to think twice about their support of plans to remove the black population from their native land.

Paul's arrival and involvement in the public debate tipped the balance against Cresson. A look at newspapers in towns where meetings were held tells the story. After every lecture by Cresson supporters of colonization would flood their local newspapers with letters extolling the virtues of Liberia and the work of the ACS. As was customary, the letters of support generated a stream of letters with opposing views. Stuart and Paul were quick to use this public debate to make their views known. Cresson expressed surprise that, by mid-1832, he had begun to run into opposition even in private meetings and suspected that Stuart and Paul were providing these closely controlled meetings with information. In Derby, for instance, he was forced to address Paul's claim that the society had been formed with the express purpose of removing the free black population from America. Cresson's response was to blame the opposition on Garrison and a handful of free blacks. Ever since the start of his mission Cresson had been concerned that the society's publications and the speeches of its leaders afforded the opposition ample ammunition with which to undermine the cause. In letters home he seemed even to be calling on the society to promote the sort of gradualist emancipation schemes that had been adopted in the West Indies, including the allowance of religious instruction and the institution of legal marriages. When in early 1832 the Birmingham Anti Slavery Society refused to meet with him and Wilberforce and Clarkson declined to sign a memorial from Cirencester supporters, Cresson thought he saw signs the tide had turned. His worst fears were confirmed once Paul had joined the fray and was vigorously promoting Wilberforce as an alternative. "I think it deserves consideration," he wrote home, "whether the awful consequences which may spring from the Canadian Colony if patronized to any extent, and which Paul . . . is now urging upon the Government ought not to be pointed out by you." The "lying mulatto preacher," as he derisively dismissed Paul, nonetheless drove Cresson to distraction, and he called on the society to challenge Paul's legitimacy by commissioning a black American to tour Britain in support of Liberia. Nothing came of the suggestion. Cresson's sense of isolation was palpable by the summer of 1832: "If, in my zeal to serve the cause, I had written or spoken . . . ought amiss . . . why not frankly tell me so? Why not as a *brother,* set me right?" But Cresson's pleas fell on deaf ears, and he hinted at plans to return home soon.[5]

Garrison's arrival in the summer of 1833 only added to Cresson's sense of profound isolation from both the society's leaders and British abolitionists. Anthony Barker argues that Cresson had been "brought to the brink of defeat by the time of Garrison's arrival." Although he underestimates the contributions of Paul to the result, he is right in his assessment of Stuart's impact, namely, that Cresson had been confronted by "two years of sustained harassment by a determined lobbyist."[6] Cresson had also to face the pointed criticism of the ACS by Garrison's widely distributed screed *Thoughts on African Colonization,* which arrived in Britain several months before Garrison did. Paul wrote of the widespread public approval of the book's arguments and regretted that it had not arrived sooner.[7]

Within days of his arrival Garrison, following the line of attack used by Stuart and Paul, challenged Cresson to a public debate on the merits of the ACS. Cresson found himself in a quandary: he could either accept a challenge that he stood little chance of winning, inasmuch as public sentiment had already grown hostile to colonization, or decline and leave the stage completely free to his opponents. When Cresson refused to accept the challenge, Garrison, with the assistance of Cropper, Stuart, Paul, and Thompson, organized a series of high-profile meetings in which they accused their opponent, among other things, of raising money under false pretenses. Cresson's refusal to confront his opponents in a public forum eroded his support even further. "We are reluctant to give up our good opinion of Mr. Cresson's motives," one editor declared, "but his proceedings are fast alienating from him those who have given him the most substantial proofs of being friends to Liberia, but who are enemies of injustice and deception." Another editor simply dismissed him as a charlatan.[8]

Cresson's problems were made worse when, in August 1833, Cropper, Thomas Fowell Buxton, Zachary Macaulay, William Smith, George Stephens, William Allen, Wilberforce, and other leading lights in British abolitionism signed a "Protest" against the ACS. It said little new, but it drove home the point that to many in the antislavery movement, the society had become anathema. The Protest was, as Garrison declared, "a millstone around the neck of the American Colonization Society, sufficiently weighty to drown it in an ocean of public indignation." The fact that Wilberforce died soon after signing it made it, in the words of Betty Fladeland, "a document worthy of veneration by abolitionists everywhere."[9] One name that was conspicuously absent from the Protest, however, was that of Clarkson. Garrison and Paul made a trip to Norwich to try to persuade him to add his name to it. Although they were unsuccessful, Clarkson made it quite clear that his initial support for the society had been extorted by Cresson's statement that "one hundred thousand slaves had been offered to the Society gratuitously, to be sent to Liberia."[10]

Rather than face the opposition on the grounds they chose, Cresson countered with the formation of the British American Colonization Society (BACS), whose founding meeting was attended by a disappointingly small number of supporters. In contrast, his opponents' public meeting at Exeter Hall attracted a crowd in excess of two thousand, among them Daniel O'Connell, the leader of the Irish Repeal movement and a longtime abolitionist, who roundly condemned the society and all supporters of slavery. The BACS was a society in name only, although its major supporter, Dr. Thomas Hodgkin, would remain the voice of colonization in Britain for much of the nineteenth century. Cresson returned home deeply affected by his experiences in Britain. Not only had he lost much of the support he had worked so hard to garner, but he also felt betrayed and abandoned by the officers of the society, especially its secretary, Ralph Gurley. He did manage to raise over two thousand pounds and enough support in Scotland to finance the establishment of a settlement in Liberia later named Edina in honor of the city which had contributed so much to the cause. But by the end of his two-and-a-half-year stay in Britain he was a spent force. At the end of it all, he lamented, he "very often felt, when thus surrounded by enemies of the fiercest stamp that unless I had been supported by the consciousness of performing an imperative and holy duty for the good of man, and the extension of the Redeemer's kingdom, that I must have been utterly overwhelmed."[11]

Garrison returned home with a copy of the Protest, in many ways a statement of how pivotal anticolonization was to the forging of the transatlantic movement. Opposition to the ACS would continue to be one of the few issues around which abolitionists of different persuasions could coalesce in the antebellum period. Not until the late 1850s would British abolitionists again show a keen interest in schemes to settle black Americans in Africa and then only because of a growing concern about Britain's almost total reliance on the South for its supply of cotton. But this was the exception. Even in the midst of the deep divisions on display at the World Anti Slavery Convention of 1840, American abolitionists in London for the meeting continued to speak with one voice against colonization. By presenting a united front on this issue, American visitors, including James G. Birney, James B. Stanton, Charles Lenox Remond, and Garrison, were able to paper over differences that otherwise could have paralyzed the international movement. Remond told a Glasgow audience, for instance, that the society was founded for the express purpose of removing the free black population from America. America, the land of boasted democracy and freedom, had never allowed blacks the liberty of choosing. The ACS was designed and organized to protect the interests of slaveholders. It afforded a place for "those who were ashamed to say, on the one hand, they were in favor of slavery, and who were equally ashamed to say they were abolitionists; these people were glad to call themselves colonization men, and thus they cut both ways."[12]

The Americans' efforts were made easier by the unfortunately timed arrival of Ralph R. Gurley in July 1840. Gurley and supporters of his mission were anxious to exploit an apparent upsurge of interest in African colonization represented by the formation of the African Civilization Society (AFCS), led by Buxton and intent on regaining ground lost by Cresson seven years earlier. The AFCS proposed to establish a string of settlements along the coast of West Africa headed by small groups of trained West Indians who would provide the native peoples of the region a legitimate commercial alternative to the slave trade as well as introduce them to Christianity. Gurley could be forgiven if he saw no differences between the two societies. But anticolonizationist sentiment had put down deep roots since Cresson's visit. As a result, Buxton thought it best to stay clear of any association with the ACS. Although following a meeting with Buxton, Gurley was optimistic that the societies could work together, his hopes were soon dashed when Buxton issued a public statement denouncing the work of the ACS in Liberia. Buxton insisted that, unlike the ACS, the AFCS aimed not to colonize but to civilize Africa. It did not intend to become master of "the resources of that continent, but to teach its natives their use and value, not to procure an outlet for any portion of our surplus population, but to show to Africa the folly as well as the crime of exporting her own children." The settlements were meant to be a secure space for the introduction of schools, agriculture, and commerce. The society had no intention of expatriating a large number of people to Africa, only a select few who would act as a "leaven amongst her people."[13] Gurley could be forgiven for thinking that the distinction did not add up to much of a difference.

Gurley also hoped to persuade British abolitionists that their earlier rejection of the ACS had been precipitous and based largely on inaccurate information. The British and Foreign Antislavery Society agreed to Gurley's request for a meeting and appointed a subcommittee to meet with him, then promptly undermined any chance for reconciliation by inviting Birney and Stanton to attend. Not surprisingly, the committee recommended against support for the ACS.[14] Gurley returned home with nothing to show for his efforts. Ten years later Cresson would again visit Britain, but on this occasion he eschewed any public debate and made few attempts to contact British abolitionists.

Garrison was understandably proud of his contributions to the defeat of colonization on both his first and second visits to Britain, even if, in retrospect, he tended to overlook the contributions of others. Defeating Cresson, after all, had been one of the declared purposes of his first visit. But his brief tour of Britain in 1833 had even greater significance for the wider transatlantic abolitionist movement. Even before leaving home he sensed that the visit had the potential to establish contacts that would benefit the fledgling movement in the United States. But he also realized that such contacts would lend international legitimacy to his position as the preeminent figure in the American movement. It was, as Duncan Rice has argued, the first attempt to "organize British sympathizers in explicit support of the American campaign." "There I shall breathe freely," Garrison wrote his wife just before leaving, "there, my sentiments and language on the subject of slavery will receive the acclamation of the people — there, my spirit will be elevated and strengthened in the presence of Clarkson, and Wilberforce, and Brougham, and Buxton, and O'Connell." Garrison proved as good as his word. During the visit he was introduced to most of the major figures in the British movement, shared platforms with the likes of O'Connell, sat in the gallery of the House of Commons during the debate over passage of the West Indian emancipation act, made a trip to meet Clarkson, met with an ailing Wilberforce and when, soon after their meeting, Wilberforce died, attended his funeral. He never tired of telling the story that at their first meeting Buxton was surprised to find that Garrison was not a black man. It seemed a fitting tribute to the passion and commitment Garrison brought to the fight against slavery.[15]

Here is how Garrison assessed the value of his trip for the campaign in America: he had awakened interest in the cause and secured support for it; he had put to rest the efforts of the ACS to distract the attention of British philanthropists; he had enlisted a committed group of advocates; he had fixed the gaze of British editors on American slavery; he had persuaded female antislavery societies to give attention and support to the plight of the American slave; and he had brought back with him a considerable collection of pamphlets, tracts, and other antislavery documents that will be of considerable use.[16] Modesty was not one of Garrison's weaknesses. Yet one cannot ignore the significance of the connections he and others forged, connections that would be strengthened further by the separate visits of Stuart and Thompson to the United States in 1834. Stuart brought with him one thousand dollars, collected to support a proposed manual labor school for African Americans. Unfortunately, local resistance to the school stymied plans for its establishment in Connecticut. Thompson brought with him books and expressions of support for Prudence Crandall, whose efforts to integrate her school for girls had met stiff resistance from opponents of the plan. Thompson's visit was the more significant of the two. He spent the next few months crisscrossing the Northeast and Midwest, holding meetings promoting the cause. His visit ran into stringent opposition almost from the beginning. There was no middle ground. To opponents he was the "mad missionary" bent on destroying the compact that held the country together; to supporters he was a force for the expansion of abolitionist sentiment. By the time of his departure Thompson had won almost universal acclaim from abolitionists and stinging condemnation from antiabolitionists.[17] In the view of the opposition Thompson's tour raised the specter of a foreign plot to destroy the country, a theme that would dog efforts by British abolitionists to promote the cause in the United States in the future.

By the time of his second visit to attend the World Anti Slavery Convention in 1840 Garrison was a household name among British abolitionists. But there were also some troubling signs that all was not well with the movement. Disputes over such contentious issues as the role of women had produced deep divisions among American abolitionists. Just weeks before the start of the convention those opposed to granting leadership roles to women had walked out of the annual meeting of the American Anti Slavery Society (AASS) in New York and formed the American and Foreign Anti Slavery Society (AFASS). These divisions had also begun to stir passions in Britain. Stuart, for one, had all but broken rank with Garrison over the ways women should participate in the movement. Others in the British and Foreign Anti Slavery Society (BFASS) seemed to have taken a similar position on the issue. Joseph Sturge, the inspiration behind the formation of the BFASS, had made the society's position abundantly clear in a letter made public in May: "It is reported that several of our female friends to the cause, are likely to be appointed from America. . . . I fear such a step would be any thing rather than a help to our cause. . . . In all our labors in this country, they held their meetings and committees perfectly distinct from ours, and the idea of appointing any female delegates to the coming Convention, will never, I believe, occur to one of the Committee in this country."[18] The point could not have been made more explicit.

Formed a year earlier and dedicated to the struggle against slavery wherever it existed, the BFASS was the driving force behind the convention. Its call for associations to send delegates to the convention generated strong interest among both factions of the American movement. Among the delegates associated with the AFASS were Birney, Stanton, and Elizabeth Cady Stanton; James and Lucretia Mott and Wendell Phillips had remained with the AASS. Garrison, Remond, William Adam, and N. P. Rogers arrived days after the opening session of the convention. By the time of their arrival the issue of women's participation had already been resolved. At the opening session, Phillips, well aware that the organizers had amended the call limiting participation to "gentlemen," had called for the establishment of a committee to prepare a list of all participants with credentials. Phillips's motion produced a spirited debate on whether women should be recognized as delegates. Stuart, in opposing the motion, said he was acquainted with many of the leading abolitionists in Pennsylvania and Massachusetts and all of them were against the "reception of lady delegates." Thompson tried unsuccessfully to mediate the dispute. In the end the convention voted not to seat the women delegates from the United States. In protest they retreated to the gallery of the hall, to what Duncan Rice nicely calls their "philanthropic purdah." In spite of efforts by the organizers to have him join the meeting on the floor, Garrison opted to join the American women delegates in the galleries.[19]

Assessing the impact of the convention, Garrison wrote his wife, "On the score of respectability, talent, and numbers, it deserves much consideration; but it was sadly deficient in freedom of thought, speech, and action, having been under the exclusive management of the London Committee, whose dominion was recognized as absolute." Phillips, who earlier had optimistically declared that the appeals of British Christians were the "sheet anchors of our cause," was now, in the wake of the convention, slightly more pessimistic. Of one thing he was now sure: British abolitionists would in the future have to take sides in the American dispute.[20]

At the close of the convention three groups of American abolitionists set off on tours of the country: one consisted of the Motts, Sarah Pugh, and Abbey Kimber; another, Birney and the Stantons; and the third, Garrison, Rogers, Remond, and Adam. The itinerary of Garrison and his group took them to cities such as Edinburgh, Glasgow, Sheffield, and Dublin, where they lectured on antislavery and temperance. In London, Garrison shared the platform at a temperance meeting with O'Connell. He also spoke at an India Reform meeting, insisting that, in the long run, the promotion of the cultivation of free-labor cotton in India would aid the cause of emancipation in the United States. It is not that Garrison was in favor of the free-labor movement. In fact, he had always been skeptical of the movement's ability to undermine slavery. But he was also deeply committed to the proposition that the wider the call for freedom throughout the world, the greater the chances of winning freedom for the slaves at home. As he told the India Reform meeting, "We should, as nations, reciprocate rebukes."[21]

In Glasgow, Garrison and the others were challenged by a group supporting workers' rights who accused the organizers of the meeting of paying attention to the needs of slaves on faraway plantations while ignoring those of workers in nearby mills. Like so many of his peers, Garrison had always rejected the notion that the experiences of slaves and workers were in any way identical. Yet, surprisingly, he responded to the workers' protest by criticizing those "who were so ready to denounce American slavery, [but who] refused to give any countenance to measures at home for the relief and elevation of the laboring classes." Local Chartists thought his response, which called on working-men and -women to improve themselves and avoid the consumption of alcohol, fell far short of the mark. Long after Garrison had returned home, others in his group continued to face challenges from British workers. James Mott reported that Chartists took over an India Reform meeting in Glasgow at which Thompson was to speak. Lucretia Mott tried to address the meeting but was refused by the chair. Remond, however, was allowed to speak, showing, James Mott concluded, that "while they have a strong prejudice against listening to the expostulations or exhortations of women, they have not the unholy prejudice against color."[22]

Garrison's assessment of the results of his second visit was radically different from that of his first and in many ways shows the extent to which differences in the movement had hardened. Gone was the optimism he had displayed at the end of his first trip. Now, he reported to Henry C. Wright, his colleague in the Non-Resistance Society, "we 'sifted into' the minds of those with whom we came in contact, all sorts of 'heresies' and 'extraneous topics,' in relation to Temperance, Non-Resistance, Moral Reform, Human Rights, Holiness, etc. etc."[23] Such heresies were only likely to widen the divisions. The unanimity apparent in the wake of Cresson's defeat in 1833 had, by the time of Garrison's return home in 1840, been replaced by a narrowing and splintering of the international alliance.

Yet Garrison's departure afforded a respite from the conflict. Remond stayed behind on an extended tour, although in the weeks immediately after Garrison's departure he had spent time in Scotland recovering from a bout of illness. During the next eighteen months, until his return to the United States in December 1841, Remond committed himself to an exhaustive lecture tour. In early 1841, for instance, he spoke on twenty-three of thirty nights on slavery, temperance, prejudice, and colonization. Only the loss of his voice forced him to suspend the tour temporarily. His work in Ireland was particularly impressive. His lectures in Belfast were attended by crowds in excess of three thousand. The growth of interest in the movement in Cork was attributed almost entirely to the work he did in that city. Years later when Douglass visited Cork he reported home that Remond's efforts "were abundant and very effective. He is spoken of here in terms of high approbation; and his name is held in affectionate remembrance by many whose hearts were warmed into life on this question by his soul-searching eloquence."[24]

But all was not smooth sailing. On his return home Garrison discovered that the split in the movement which had occurred just before he sailed for London had left the AASS almost penniless. The dire financial conditions were made worse by the loss of the *Emancipator,* the society's newspaper, which was taken over, some say illegally, by those who had bolted. Money had to be found to keep the society afloat. As a result, the decision was made to send John A. Collins, a Vermont abolitionist, on a mission to raise funds from supporters in Britain. His arrival reignited tensions that, since the convention, had been relatively muted. Collins was not noted for subtleness or finesse. He chose to present the difficulty over the *Emancipator* as a matter of theft and tried to force the BFASS to take sides on the matter. The society initially ignored him and refused to have any communication with him. The isolation irritated Collins, who dismissed British abolitionists as "laced up in sectarian jackets, and screwed up like the bride in the ballroom, unable to dance to the music." Stuart insisted, and the society agreed, that support for the agent of the "women-intruding" party would do nothing to aid the cause of antislavery in the United States. If Collins made no headway with the society in London he had better luck in Glasgow and Dublin, where his efforts led to the decision of the Glasgow Emancipation Society and the Hibernian Anti Slavery Society to throw in their lot with the Garrisonians.[25]

Remond did what he could to avoid becoming embroiled in these squabbles and initially refused to join Collins. But he was limited in what he could do. He was, after all, a prominent member of the AASS, one who had made his allegiances unmistakably clear. Some, such as Birney, thought this limited his effectiveness in Britain. But Remond insisted that he could remain an ally of Garrison and still be able to work with the BFASS. He did criticize the London society for adopting what he thought was an unnecessarily narrow view of the AASS. Nonresistance, he pointed out, was not the majority view of the members of the AASS. The two can and should be separated. He, for instance, had never attended a nonresistance meeting, yet he remained a strong supporter of the society. He cautioned Collins to avoid "open warfare" with the BFASS, offering explanations of his position only when asked directly about it. Thompson reported that Remond had adopted a "line of conduct" that was free of partisanship but allowed him "the opportunity of vindicating his friends whenever unjustly treated." He worked closely with the Belfast Anti Slavery Society, well aware it had thrown its support to those opposed to Garrison. "I have with *simplicity of manner*," he wrote Elizabeth Pease, "enjoyed visiting and dining and teaing with a number of families doubly interesting from their high new organization position."[26]

Collins returned home in July 1841 with nothing to show for his efforts. He was forced to borrow money from Phillips to pay for his return ticket. Collins had little good to say about British abolitionists. "They can talk about slavery," he told Garrison, "because they have never been corrupted by its presence upon their own soil. The English can never condemn our prejudice against color, our negro seats and negro cars, while they are exercising the same prejudice against poverty, that we do against color. It is unphilosophical to think that the British people as a nation should be in favor of genuine freedom."[27] If nothing else, Collins's experiences in Britain had set him on a course toward socialism.

All was not totally lost, however. Before leaving for home, Collins and Remond had begun discussions in Dublin with the Hibernian Anti Slavery Society (HASS) about the possibility of drawing up an address from Ireland to Irish immigrants in the United States calling on them to join the fight against slavery. It was left to Remond to promote the idea in the fall of 1841. Wherever he went on his extensive lecture tour of Ireland he found support for the proposed address. This was no mean accomplishment given that the attention of the people had been almost totally consumed by the movement for Irish repeal from the British Union. The collection of names to what became known as the Irish Address was administered by the HASS, led by Richard Webb, Richard Allen, and James Haughton. By the time of Remond's return home, sixty thousand people had affixed their name to the address, which called on Irish immigrants to join forces with the abolitionists to destroy slavery and to work for the elimination of discrimination against blacks. "Irishmen and Irishwomen!" it declared. "Treat the colored people as your equal, as brethren." Among its signatories were O'Connell and Father Theobold Mathew, the leader of the Irish temperance movement.[28]

Unlike the Protest which Garrison brought back in 1833, the Irish Address had the potential to generate considerable support for those fighting against slavery. But given the experiences of Thompson in 1834 it also carried increased risks for a movement that had always been suspected of doing the work of foreigners. Within weeks of Remond's return the address was unveiled at a meeting at Faneuil Hall, Boston, attended by five thousand, including a fair number of Irishmen, although it is not clear exactly how many were in attendance. The organizers of the meeting estimated that the number was substantial; opponents thought otherwise. Whatever the case, the address met with instant and sustained opposition. There were those who questioned its authenticity, and others who doubted that O'Connell would have signed such a call. The two Boston newspapers that catered to Irish immigrants sneered at the address. In New York City, Bishop John Hughes questioned its authenticity and called on Irishmen to repudiate what he saw as foreign interference in the domestic affairs of the country. Others rejected the attempt to appeal to them as a group distinct from all others in the country. They were, they insisted, Americans devoted to the maintenance of the Union and opposed to any effort that could disrupt that compact. Moreover, there were those who were stunned by the call to treat the colored people as equals. That, they insisted, smacked of amalgamation.[29]

That anyone who knew the history of O'Connell's position on slavery would doubt his support of the Irish Address stunned Garrison and other American abolitionists. To them the alliance between abolition and repeal seemed natural. Irish American Repealers begged to differ. They should avoid, at all cost, attaching themselves to any other cause, especially one promoted from abroad. Their attachment to the American Constitution was so deep and controlling that they could not be expected to do anything that would imperil "the only free government in the world." Faced with such widespread opposition Phillips called on Irish supporters to persuade O'Connell to send "us a startling scorching bitter unsparing, pointed rebuke." But friends in Dublin were not optimistic. Besides the level of opposition that the address had generated, Webb worried that O'Connell was not up to the task and warned that he should not be trusted. O'Connell had to confront two difficult questions from American supporters. Why, they asked, should they give their support to a movement that wished to destroy the Union by sowing rebellion among slaves? And why should they support those who promoted such radical ideas as the questioning of the Sabbath? O'Connell's response was to restate his commitment to abolition and at the same time condemn Garrison, who on matters of religion, he said, was "something of a maniac." To Webb, O'Connell was "either a great bigot or a rank hypocrite. . . . In his last abolition speech . . . he meanly throws a sop to Cerberus by denouncing Garrison as 'a Mr. Lloyd Garrison with whom he could have no intercourse' on account of his religious or rather irreligious opinions." Webb dismissed O'Connell's speeches as full of "excitement, inflammatory eloquence, and mere swagger."[30]

Garrison was understandably hurt by O'Connell's accusation and public dismissal. But the Irish leader was under considerable pressure both from American supporters to distance himself from the abolitionists and from forces at home who totally rejected his insistence on coupling repeal and abolition. Some in America threatened to withhold funds, others talked of disbanding repeal societies in protest. In response to these competing pressures, O'Connell adopted an approach that allowed him to continue to call for the abolition of slavery, to criticize those who opposed the movement, and yet accept support from America. He recognized, too, that repealers were under enormous pressure from opponents, who charged them with all sorts of plots, from attempts to influence the outcome of elections to colluding with the Catholic Church and abolitionists to destroy the country. O'Connell's approach gave him the flexibility to continue issuing blistering condemnations of American slavery and those who supported it, as he did in response to the declarations of a Cincinnati repeal meeting in May 1843. In doing so he kept alive the debate over slavery among Irish Americans. And Garrisonians may have continued to express outrage at O'Connell's barbs, but his unwavering stand against slavery made him an asset in the effort to win Irish Americans to the cause. In the two years after the arrival of the address the issue would flare anew every time O'Connell issued a statement against slavery. While the hoped for alliance that the address promised never materialized, O'Connell remained a vital force in the transatlantic movement until his death in 1847. "Despite his disavowal of them," Douglas Riach has argued, Garrisonians "issued pamphlets of his speeches, and, after his death, made appeals to his memory."[31]

The failure of the World Anti Slavery Convention and its organizers, the BFASS, to bring under the umbrella of antislavery all who were opposed to slavery regardless of the views they may have espoused on other subjects frustrated Garrison. Collins's inability to make much headway confirmed his worst fears. By the end of 1841 Garrison's British support was limited to a network of relatively small societies in Glasgow, Dublin, and Edinburgh. These were later joined by associations in Bristol and Leeds. Soon after the convention a small group of Boston nonresisters floated the idea of a "World's Convention for the discussion of all wrongs," to be held somewhere in Britain. Given that Britain was in a "singularly plastic and reformatory state," as Garrison put it, a mission to rally support for the meeting seemed logical. The commission fell to Henry C. Wright. Some dismissed the idea as preposterous and the choice of the person to appeal for support even stranger. Lydia Maria Child wondered why Wright of all people was selected: "He appears to me as little calculated to do good as almost any person they could select." Given the "heresies" he and Garrison were so fond of promoting, it would have been a surprise had Wright been any more successful than Collins. In spite of his commission Wright spent most of his time lecturing on slavery. The idea of a new and radically different convention never got off the ground. Wherever he went controversy followed. "No one orchestrated religious hatred more zealously than Wright," Lewis Perry has argued, "no one leveled more dramatically phrased charges, no one occasioned more fury."[32]

If the convention of 1840 had frustrated Garrisonians, its call to British churches to refuse fellowship with slaveholders and American churches that condoned slavery was the sort of declaration around which both wings of the movement could rally. They were handed an issue when a commission from the recently established Free Church of Scotland returned from a tour of the United States with money, some of which, it was suspected, was raised in the South. The Free Church had been established in the wake of the Scottish Disruption of 1843. Funds were desperately needed to build churches and pay ministers. Soon after the return of the commission, Wright, the Glasgow Emancipation Society (GES), a supporter of Garrison, and the Belfast Anti Slavery Society (BASS), an affiliate of the BFASS, launched a public campaign that aimed to force the church to "Send Back the Money." Wright was joined by Douglass and James Buffum in the fall of 1845. The campaign against the Free Church would consume their energies for almost one year. First they attempted to pressure the Presbyterian Church in Belfast to sever its connections with the Free Church until the money was returned. When that approach failed to have the desired effect, they took their message to Scotland. What followed was a vitriolic public debate which caused deep divisions in the new church and almost bankrupted the GES. In Paisley, Douglass accused the church of lining its pockets with money that any morally grounded organization would have committed instead to his education. He called on his audiences to raise their voices against the church. Let the issue, he pleaded, be "the talk around the fireside, in the streets, and at the market-place." This call for public agitation struck some as particularly dangerous to social order and indirectly may have won the church support. In the end the Free Church held its ground and defied the call to return the money. Even in failure Buffum took comfort in the prediction that the agitation would lead to a greater understanding of the nature of American slavery.[33]

Garrison arrived in July 1846 and for the next three months would add his voice to the campaign to isolate American churches. But before joining Douglass, Thompson, and the others on a lecture tour, Garrison turned his attention to the formation of the Anti Slavery League. It was meant to be a counterweight to the BFASS, an organization that could give national voice to the provincial societies that had kept faith with Garrison. The founding meeting at the Crown & Anchor on August 10, 1846, attracted many of the leading British Garrisonians as well as a number of radicals such as the Chartist Henry Vincent. The success of the meeting lifted Garrison's spirits. The league, he predicted, would make a "deep impression on the public mind, on both sides of the Atlantic." Others were not so optimistic. In fact, there were those such as John B. Estlin, the Bristol ophthalmologist, who thought Garrison had undermined his chances of winning support by associating with political fringe elements, those willing to divide the country by promoting a series of impractical movements such as universal suffrage, and the unsavory characters like Vincent who promoted them. "Were the middle and lower classes of this country the parties likely to do much for the American Abolitionist cause," he warned Garrison, "there might be some use in courting their favour, even at the risk of offending higher circles."[34]

In the weeks after the Anti Slavery League's formation, Garrison, Douglass, Thompson, Wright, and Buffum continued their effort to isolate American churches. Although they kept up the demand for the Free Church to return the money it had raised in the South, much of their attention was devoted to the proposed Evangelical Alliance, which many of its proponents hoped would cement contacts between British and American evangelicals. From the outset questions were raised about the exact nature, function, and composition of the alliance. Sectarian differences and national jealousies complicated what was already a difficult situation. In the end, the organizers opted for breadth and flexibility, hopeful that the founding meeting could unravel the many problems created by its rules of association. A preliminary meeting of British evangelicals in Birmingham had voted not to extend an invitation to those in America who "whether by their own fault or otherwise, may be in the unhappy position of holding their fellowmen as slaves." The resolution arrived too late to affect the composition of the American delegation. The issue of whether slaveholders could be members consumed the energies of the meeting and in the end destroyed the hopes of a united alliance. They opted instead for the formation of national organizations "in accordance with their peculiar circumstances, without involving the responsibility of one part of the Alliance for another."[35]

Given the passions unleashed by the debate over the Free Church's acceptance of money from the South, the Evangelical Alliance stood little chance of succeeding. British delegates were committed to the cause of abolition even if, like the Reverend J. Howard Hinton, they had rejected Garrison's approach. It is this antislavery tradition that Garrison, Douglass, and Thompson called upon in their public meetings in the days after the formation of the league. Judging by the audiences they attracted and the support they were given wherever they went, their call for the isolation of American churches seemed to resonate with large sections of the British public. They also took the message to the World Temperance Convention, which met in London not long after the alliance meeting. Many of the Americans in London for the alliance meeting stayed on for the convention and, not surprisingly, were incensed by the attempt to raise the issue at the meeting. While Garrison's intervention was summarily rejected by the chair, Douglass, who attended as an accredited delegate from Newcastle, was allowed to address the meeting. Besides pointing to the fact that no American association would have considered electing him as its representative, Douglass devoted much of his address to the ways discrimination undermined the attempts of free blacks to elevate themselves. By the end of the summer, many Americans at the meetings were convinced of the existence of a coalition of American and British abolitionists whose purpose, one of them observed, was to fan the flames of "national exasperation and war."[36]

As he had done at the end of his two previous visits to Britain, Garrison declared this visit a rousing success. "Nothing could have been more timely," he told a coworker, "no three months of my life were ever spent more profitably to the cause of religious and personal freedom."[37] But as much as their agitation excited public interest it could not ensure the survival of the league, which languished in the months after Garrison's departure. It was not for a want of trying. For the rest of his stay in Britain Douglass continued to promote the cause, but in Garrison's absence what Douglass did raised his own stock rather than the league's. Not only did he become the center of attraction, but, like Remond before him, Douglass saw no reason why he should forgo contacts with the BFASS and its supporters if those contacts would strengthen the movement. Such independence caused Webb to question Douglass's allegiances. "I have not found him as agreeable as I would wish," Webb wrote Wright. "I don't at all feel confident that his head will be strong enough for the attention he receives." When Douglass accepted an invitation to meet with the BFASS Webb was beside himself. He wrote Maria W. Chapman in Boston, "I don't wonder at Douglass' having met with the British and Foreign as he has done. It must be difficult for him to enter into your feelings in this matter, and he is not a man to enter into what he don't comprehend." Sturge, the leader of the BFASS, Webb observed, is "shuffling, secretive, bigoted and destitute of magnanimity but he is benevolent and munificent, and it is only in these latter phases of his character that Douglass has seen him."[38]

Douglass was not the problem; Webb had difficulty with anyone who ignored his advice. Other Garrisonians took a different view of the meeting. Thompson supported the idea, and from America the Reverend Samuel May Jr. thought that the offer to meet with Douglass showed a willingness on the part of the BFASS to "let a friend" of the AASS have "free speech on their platform." He also thought Douglass might take the opportunity to correct some errors.[39] Webb's reaction is all the more surprising given that, like Remond, Douglass took every opportunity to publicly declare his allegiance to Garrison. At a meeting in Leeds in December, for instance, he made his position clear: "I like Joseph Sturge of Birmingham. I revere the Anti-Slavery Committee. I love the abolitionists of England; but they ask of me too much when they desire me to step down from the side of Garrison. Sacrifice the man from whom I have received more than from any man breathing—my first, my last, my most steadfast friend—the friend of liberty, the great parent of freedom. Impossible!"[40]

The problem for the Garrisonian movement in Britain was not the insistence of African Americans such as Remond and Douglass that they had a right to meet with anyone who supported the cause, but the choice of agents the AASS chose to send to Britain. After each of their visits, Garrison's supporters in Britain seem to go further into their shell, convinced that others were undermining the cause. It took some persuasion to get Remond to agree to work with Collins. Douglass was equally reluctant to join forces with Wright. "Friend Wright," he wrote Webb, "is identified with doctrines for which I do not wish to be responsible. He is truly a reformer in general; I only claim to be a man of one idea."[41] Douglass was being uncharacteristically coy, but his point was well made: the heresies that Wright and Garrison were so fond of seemed to work against the declared aim of winning British support for abolition. Remond and Douglass were not naïve. They were aware that the BFASS, particularly its secretary, John Scoble, was committed to a policy of isolating the Garrisonians. In spite of their willingness to keep the door of communication ajar, such public declarations of support for Garrison as Douglass's should have eased Webb's concerns and discomforted Scoble.

As if prefiguring the famous Monty Python skit, British Garrisonians had developed a tendency to pull up the drawbridge, retreat into the safety of their sectarian castle, and shout abuse at potential intruders from the parapets. But this siege mentality was not totally misplaced. Webb could see, as others could not, that Douglass might replace Garrison in the hearts of British supporters of the movement. Within a few years, his worst fears were confirmed. Douglass broke with Garrison, established his own newspaper, and continued to attract financial support from a growing number of people who found Garrison much too radical for their abolitionist tastes. By 1850 many in Garrisonian strongholds were drifting away. In Glasgow, for instance, a new ladies' society called on the public to transfer its support from Boston to those who were helping slaves escape to Canada because they had grown weary of people like Wright who set aside, one wrote, the authenticity of the Old Testament in order "to controvert the arguments of proslavery Professors of Christianity."[42] Many believed the new societies in Scotland were the work of the African American Reverend J. W. C. Pennington. The period also witnessed the revitalization of the apparently anti-Garrisonian Free Produce Movement, which called for a boycott of slave-grown produce. Finally, the success of Harriet Beecher Stowe's tour in 1853 deepened the Garrisonians' sense of isolation.

African American Garrisonians like William Wells Brown and William and Ellen Craft, who visited Britain in the 1850s, met with similar criticism when they accepted invitations from the BFASS. But the problem for British Garrisonians was not the flexibility that African Americans insisted on, but the intractability of their white American visitors. No one raised the levels of bile like Parker Pillsbury, the New Hampshire abolitionist. Some could forgive Wright's oddities, but Pillsbury was simply too cantankerous. In the two and a half years he spent in Britain Pillsbury managed to cross swords with anyone who deviated from what he considered the only legitimate approach to abolition. He was particularly incensed by the activities of a group of African American ministers including Pennington, Henry Highland Garnet, Samuel Ward, and Josiah Henson, whom he accused of "picking the people's pockets." That fry, as he dismissed them, were "an outrage on all decency and a scandal to the name of anti-slavery." They were the Garrisonians' major competitors as far as Pillsbury was concerned. Pennington's success at getting supporters to raise money to purchase his freedom "prevents or perverts the gifts that would be cheerfully laid on the altar of humanity, by representing things to be antislavery which are not, and runs away with the sympathies of a generous people, who really wish well of the cause of the slave." Later Pillsbury would become involved in the whispered campaign which raised questions of an illicit sexual relationship between Douglass and his coworker the Englishwoman Julia Griffiths, who had returned from Rochester to her home country in 1855 to raise support for Douglass's work.[43]

These difficulties are all the more unfortunate given that Pillsbury's arrival in Britain coincided with a change of leadership in the BFASS. Its old secretary, Scoble, the Garrisonians' nemesis, had been replaced by Louis Chamerovzow, a courtly Polish immigrant, who on assuming the position made efforts to heal the rift by inviting Pillsbury, Thompson, and Brown to the society's annual meeting. The gesture proved a disaster. After some hesitation, Pillsbury agreed to attend the meeting, but he had no intention of allowing the society to make public noises about reconciliation without first declaring the AASS the true abolitionists. The invitation raised suspicions among friends at home. Samuel May Jr. insisted that the idea of "obtaining strength from an alliance with those who have been seeking our ruin, and in every mean and covert way, for fifteen years, is to me simply preposterous." Like other African Americans who were invited to participate in BFASS activities, Brown was partial to accepting the invitation without setting preconditions. Pillsbury was not. And when Chamerovzow refused to allow his motion Pillsbury responded, "We [must] not let the enemy get advantage by another act of pretended friendliness." There can be no reconciliation, he declared, until "their repentance is far less equivocal than any we have seen yet."[44]

This was the last meaningful attempt to reconcile the two groups. The small group of Garrisonians continued to function largely isolated from what remained of antislavery activity in Britain. Webb would write almost plaintively during Pillsbury's visit that the activities of Douglass's supporters had limited his effectiveness and his ability to raise money for the Boston bazaar. By 1858 the sale of British goods for the bazaar, which annually raised money for the work of the AASS, had all but dried up. The competition, particularly Douglass in Rochester and those in New York City and Syracuse working to help runaways escape slavery, continued, however, to attract support from Britain. When in 1858 Samuel Joseph May, a leading figure in the American movement, visited Britain he made few public appearances. He limited his activities almost exclusively to private meetings with the shrinking group of British Garrisonians. This lack of public agitation contrasted starkly with the activities of Sarah Parker Remond, Charles Lenox Remond's sister, who traveled to Britain with May. Remond undertook an active public campaign that almost single-handedly revivified Garrisonian activity in places like Leeds, where it had lain dormant for years. At the end of a visit which lasted less than a year May believed that divisions among American abolitionists had turned many in Britain against leaders of the movement.[45]

The small group of British Garrisonians may have lost much of its ability to affect public views of the movement in America, but their relative isolation did breed solidarity, a solidarity that was sorely tested by the outbreak of war in America, which surprisingly caused deep rifts in the alliance. The small, tightly knit group which had largely weathered the scorn of opponents for being extremists and cantankerous now showed signs of fraying in the months after the outbreak of hostilities. For over twenty years its members had preached, some would say to the converted, that the peaceful secession of the non-slaveholding states from the Union was the best guarantor of emancipation. Wright promoted the idea unstintingly during his stay in Britain, echoing

Garrison's declaration in the midst of the furor over the Irish Address, that he, and by extension the AASS, was both an "Irish Repealer and an American Repealer." The firing on Fort Sumter turned belief into promise. British members of the alliance, therefore, were caught off guard by the ease with which American colleagues shelved the commitment to come out in favor of supporting and staying in the Union. American friends, in turn, took umbrage at the insistence of British coworkers that the principle still held sway. From Dublin Haughton insisted that the South be allowed to leave; otherwise the conflict will lead to "extermination, or a fierce and horrible encounter of long duration." Were the South allowed to go quietly, the North would be finally freed of its complicity with slavery. Haughton drove home his argument with the pointed reminder of the movement's slogan: "No Union with Slaveholders." Friends in America defended themselves. They had never abandoned principle, for they had never rejected the concept of union, only one that was built on slavery, Phillips declared, "a union whose cement was the blood of the slave." Now that the North seemed determined to take seriously the unchallenged views which drove the Declaration of Independence and the spirit of the Revolution, union should be supported. If these beliefs prevailed, many in Britain, both in and out of the movement, wanted to know, why had Abraham Lincoln not made emancipation and the search for justice the cornerstone of the war? American colleagues could not easily answer these questions until the Preliminary Emancipation Proclamation was issued in September 1862.[46]

The squabble unleashed nationalist passions as the internationalist principles that had sustained the movement for thirty years gave way in the face of war. Harriet Martineau, one of the stalwarts of the alliance, who knew America from her first visit in the 1830s and to whose home in Ambleside every American Garrisonian who visited Britain made the obligatory pilgrimage, for a while parted company with her American friends in the movement for what she thought was their abandonment of free trade and internationalist principles. Webb, on the other hand, stayed involved, but in his usual fashion did not hold his peace in the face of what he saw as a disturbing sign of rising American nationalism. In response, some who had always been candid and open with colleagues chose to wrap themselves in the flag. One in particular reminded friends that Britain's hands were stained in the blood of one hundred thousand Sepoys, victims of the war in India: "Great as is the sin of this country, culpable as is its government, and unworthy as are its leaders, America is the peer of all other nations; and, in her recent sacrifices for liberty, without a peer among the nations of the earth. It is in comparison with our own ideal that we condemn our country as the 'chief of sinners'; but in comparison with other nations, we have no reason to be ashamed."[47]

Lincoln's Emancipation Proclamation went a long way to seal the fissures that had appeared in the transatlantic Garrisonian movement. But by that time the movement was a mere shadow of itself. Many of the stalwarts, such as J. B. Estlin, had passed from the scene, while others, such as the members of the Glasgow Emancipation Society, had become relatively inactive. Some younger voices, including Mary Estlin, daughter of John, and members of the Leeds Young Men's Anti Slavery Society, had joined the ranks only in the last decade before the war. These new voices, however, were never loud enough to replace those silenced by retirement or death. Whatever cohesion existed was a tribute to Garrison's stature and influence. After his visit to Dublin in 1840, Webb's wife, Hannah, summed it up best. Garrison was working, she said, for a "world in which there would be no slavery, no king, no beggars, no lawyers, no doctors, no soldiers, no palaces, no prisons, no creeds, no sects, no weary and grinding labor, no luxurious idleness, no particular Sabbath or temple . . . no restraint but moral restraint, no containing power but love. Shall we judge such a man because he may go a little further than we are prepared to follow? Let us first consult our consciences and our testaments."[48]

Hannah Webb may have allowed her enthusiasm for Garrison to get the better of her judgment, but no one would have challenged her declaration that Garrison held the movement together. If Hannah was willing to accept Garrison's unorthodoxy, however, the extremism of Wright and Pillsbury sometimes grated on the sensibilities of their closest friends. There were occasions when, compared to Wright, Garrison was the paragon of moderation. While Wright, for instance, condemned the plan to raise money to buy Douglass's freedom and tried to persuade Douglass to reject the offer, Garrison saw merit in the plan. Were he a runaway slave, he observed, under constant threat of being retaken, he too would have accepted the offer. That flexibility and Garrison's visits in 1840 and 1846 were largely responsible for holding together his small transatlantic alliance. But one should not underestimate the contributions visiting African Americans made to the wider movement. More than any others they consistently tried to bridge the divide by working with those Garrisonians considered the opposition. The fact that during his three brief visits he toured with Paul in 1833, Remond in 1840, and Douglass in 1846, all of whom stayed behind to carry on the appeal for public support, points to the contributions they made to the international movement. After the split of the movement in the United States took hold in Britain toward the end of 1841, there was little Garrison could have done to stop further erosion. In the 1850s many in Britain thought Douglass was by far the most important leader of the American movement and the one to whom most support should be given. That development may help to explain the rather clumsy attempt to discredit

Douglass by Pillsbury and others, an effort Garrison admittedly did nothing to quell. Yet among those who knew its history Garrison was the initiator and remained the preeminent figure in the transatlantic movement.

Two years after the surrender of Confederate forces at Appomattox Garrison made his final visit to Britain. Thompson traveled with him, returning home after almost three years in America. It seemed fitting that the two who had cemented the alliance with Garrison's visit to Britain in 1833 and Thompson's to the United States the following year made the journey together. The visit gave Garrison an opportunity to reestablish old abolitionist friendships as well as meet many of the politicians and intellectuals who had played prominent roles in the debate over Britain's reactions to the Civil War. A breakfast in Garrison's honor in London was attended by many of the leading lights of British public life, including John Bright, John Stuart Mill, Thomas Hughes, Peter A. Taylor, and William Ashurst, at whose home Garrison had earlier met many of Europe's prominent radical figures. Also in attendance were the African Americans Sarah Parker Remond, J. Sella Martin, the Boston minister in Britain to raise money for the support of freedmen in the South, the Crafts, and Bishop Daniel Payne of the African Methodist Episcopalian Church. The mix of participants was a tribute to the search for justice and equality that drove Garrison and the movement that bore his name. But of all the prominent names attached to the list of participants none was more curious than that of the wartime foreign minister, Lord John Russell, who had asked to be invited and be allowed to speak. Russell's speech was the public confession of a person who had been highly critical of the Union's efforts to subdue the Confederacy. He used the occasion to admit that he and, by extension, the prime minister, Lord Palmerston, were wrong not to have recognized the difficulties Lincoln faced in reestablishing the authority of the Union and in freeing the slaves. But he took comfort in the fact that both the United States and Britain were now treating "the race of Africa as a free community, free to enter into the paths of industry, free to distinguish themselves in intellectual progress as much as any race of our own color." It was a remarkable declaration, one that hewed closely to nineteenth-century Anglo-Saxon notions about ways to uplift backward peoples, ignoring all that had gone on in the West Indies since the end of slavery and the terrible crises that had been unleashed in the wake of the Morant Bay Rebellion in Jamaica in October 1865, to say nothing of the Indian Mutiny in 1857.

Garrison was gracious in his reply. While he recognized there was a time when supporters of the Union marveled at "some sentiments which had fallen" from Russell's lips he attributed them in part to "misconceptions and misapprehensions" caused by distance. There was also understandable confusion given the early policies of the Lincoln administration, but once emancipation was declared, he concluded, "the pulse of England beat to the music of the jubilee bell." Like a true confessor, Garrison absolved Russell of his sins against the cause of freedom, first, by recognizing his public disavowal of his earlier position and, second, by calling on him to complete the work of freedom by giving the vote to the working people of Britain. The call for the extension of the franchise was Garrison's way of thanking those who had been the backbone of the Union cause in Britain during the war. But in many ways it was also an acknowledgment that the movement's objectives had been realized. Struggles for freedom in one place, Charles Lenox Remond was fond of saying, drew inspiration and strength from the fight for freedom by others elsewhere. Other cities joined in the tribute to Garrison. Similar events were held in Manchester, Glasgow, Edinburgh, and Newcastle-upon-Tyne.

The tribute recognized Garrison's contributions to the founding of the transatlantic alliance and confirmed his rightful place, participants agreed, as the preeminent figure in the movement. It was a movement forged in a period of high optimism as Britain worked toward emancipation in its West Indian colonies. It coalesced initially around opposition to the American Colonization Society and the mission of its emissary Elliot Cresson but quickly splintered in the wake of rising sectarian differences. By the end of Garrison's second visit the movement had divided into two mainly irreconcilable camps whose energies were devoted to either the promotion of or resistance to what both sides considered Garrisonian heresies. In spite of Remond's efforts, these struggles over conflicting ideologies resulted in the narrowing of support for the Garrison wing of the American movement. Other visiting African Americans tried, with some success, to heal the rift and to reach across the divide. By the end of his third visit and the struggle over the Free Church's acceptance of support from the South, much of Garrison's support was clustered in the provinces in such places as Glasgow, Edinburgh, and Dublin. By then he had lost the support of the BFASS, the one truly national organization. It is very likely that those who sided with Garrison after the 1840 convention were motivated in part by a deep desire to demonstrate their independence from both London and the BFASS. But if Hannah Webb spoke for others, then they were also driven by a passionate commitment to Garrison himself, a commitment that drew sustenance from their relative isolation from the main center of abolitionist activity. This growing isolation may help to explain why they were so critical of anyone who consorted with the opposition. In being so critical, Richard Webb and others failed to realize that the determination of African Americans to bridge the divide was doing much to keep the movement alive and vibrant. Some Garrisonians were more aware of the importance of

African Americans to the movement than was Webb. In fact, the decision of, first, the Bristol society and, later, the Young Men's society in Leeds to throw in their lot with Garrison was largely due to the efforts of, respectively, William Wells Brown and the Crafts and Sarah Parker Remond. If partisan differences divided the transatlantic movement in 1840 it was, ironically, nationalism that threatened the Garrisonian alliance in the early months of the Civil War. But in spite of these differences and divisions Garrison retained his position as the preeminent figure in the international movement, a stature that was challenged but never undermined by the prominence of Douglass.

Notes

1. Aileen Kraditor, *Means and Ends in American Abolitionism: Garrison and His Critics on Strategy and Tactics, 1834–1850* (New York: Pantheon Books, 1967), 27–28.

2. *Eclectic Review,* January 1832.

3. For a discussion of the "civilizationist principle," see Wilson J. Moses, "Civilizing Missionary: A Study of Alexander Crummell," *Journal of Negro History* 60, no. 2 (April 1975): 229–32; Wilberforce to Clarkson, Bath, October 10, 1831, Clarkson Papers, vol. 8, British Museum; Thompson to Jenny, Hastings, November 1, 1831, Robert English Deposit, John Rylands Library, Manchester University.

4. *Christian Advocate,* February 6, 1832; *Patriot,* August 1, July 18, 1832; for an example of Stuart's pamphlets, see Charles Stuart, *Remarks on the Colony of Liberia and the American Colonization Society: With Some Account of the Settlement of Coloured People, at Wilberforce, Upper Canada* (London: J. Messeder, 1832); Anthony J. Barker, *Captain Charles Stuart, Anglo-American Abolitionist* (Baton Rouge: Louisiana State University Press, 1983).

5. Derby *Mercury,* September 19, 1832; Cresson to Ralph R. Gurley, London, September 6, 1831, reel 12, Cresson to Gurley, Birmingham, February 20, 1832, reel 13, Cresson to Gurley, Liverpool, April 16, 1832, Cresson to Gurley, London, July 6, 1832, June 9, 1832, June 16, 1832, reel 14, American Colonization Society (ACS) Papers; R. J. M. Blackett, *Building an Antislavery Wall: Black Americans in the Atlantic Abolitionist Movement, 1830–1860* (Baton Rouge: Louisiana State University Press, 1983), 59.

6. Barker, *Captain Charles Stuart,* 75.

7. Betty Fladeland, *Men and Brothers: Anglo-American Antislavery Cooperation* (Urbana: University of Illinois Press, 1972), 212; *Liberator,* June 22, 1833.

8. *Patriot,* July 10, 1833; Sheffield *Iris,* July 3, 1833.

9. *Christian Advocate,* n.d., in *Liberator,* October 12, 1833; Fladeland, *Men and Brothers,* 217.

10. Wendell Phillips Garrison and Francis Jackson Garrison, *William Lloyd Garrison, 1805–1879: The Story of His Life Told by His Children,* 4 vols. (New York: Arno Press, 1969), 1:364.

11. *Liberator,* September 21, 1833; *American Antislavery Reporter,* January 1834, dismissed the BACS as "a grand castle of moonshine."

12. *American Antislavery Reporter,* October 21, November 4, 1840; *Liberator,* November 27, 1840; Ipswich *Express,* January 5, 1841.

13. *Irish Friend,* April 1, 1841; the AFCS's expedition to the Niger River in 1841 was a total failure. See Howard Temperley, *White Dreams, Black Africa: The Antislavery Expedition to the Niger River 1841–1842* (New Haven: Yale University Press, 1991).

14. Dwight L. Dumond, *Letters of James Gillespie Birney, 1831–1857,* 2 vols. (New York: Appleton-Century, 1938), 2:97–98.

15. Clare Taylor, ed., *British and American Abolitionists: An Episode in Transatlantic Understanding* (Edinburgh: University of Edinburgh Press,1974), 22; Duncan Rice, *The Scots Abolitionists, 1833–1861* (Baton Rouge: Louisiana State University Press), 15.

16. *Liberator,* September 9, 1833.

17. Rice, *Scots Abolitionists,* 68–71; Garrison and Garrison, *William Lloyd Garrison,* 1:434; Taylor, *British and American Abolitionists,* 33.

18. Quoted in Walter McIntosh Merrill, *Against Wind and Tide: A Biography of Wm. Lloyd Garrison* (Cambridge: Harvard University Press, 1963), 161.

19. Garrison and Garrison, *William Lloyd Garrison,* 2:367–71; Rice, *Scots Abolitionists,* 88–89.

20. Taylor, *British and American Abolitionists,* 74, 91–92.

21. Garrison and Garrison, *William Lloyd Garrison,* 2:408.

22. Ibid., 2:400–01; *Liberator,* October 2, 1840; James Mott, *Three Months in Great Britain* (Philadelphia: J. Miller M'Kim, 1841), 64. Throughout his remaining time in Britain Remond was forced to address the issue of workingmen in his audience. On some occasions his approach seemed to have won their endorsement, while on others they continued to raise questions from the floor. See, for example, Ipswich *Express,* January 15, 1841, Gateshead *Observer,* February 6, 1841.

23. Quoted in Rice, *Scots Abolitionists,* 96.

24. *Liberator,* May 21, 1841, November 28, 1845; Remond to William Smeal, Newcastle-upon-Tyne, February 15, 1841, Cork Ladies Anti Slavery Society to the Secretary, Boston Female Anti Slavery Society, Cork, November 15, 1841, both in Anti Slavery Papers, Boston Public Library; *Irish Friend,* March 1, 1841.

25. On Collins's visit, see Rice, *Scots Abolitionists,* 97–101; Douglas C. Riach, "Richard Davis Webb and Antislavery in Ireland," in Lewis Perry and Michael Fellman, eds., *Antislavery Reconsidered: New Perspectives on the Abolitionists* (Baton Rouge: Louisiana State University Press, 1979), 158; Charles John A. Collins, *Right and Wrong Among the Abolitionists of the United States* (Glasgow: G. Gallie, 1841), 70.

26. Dumond, *Letters of James Gillespie Birney,* 2:584; Remond to Richard Allen, London, January 7, 1841, BFASS Papers, Rhodes House Library, Oxford University; Thompson to Elizabeth Pease, Edinburgh, October 27, 1840, Robert English Deposit; Remond to Elizabeth Pease, Belfast, October 14, 1841, Anti Slavery Papers.

27. Taylor, *British and American Abolitionists,* 133–34.

28. Belfast *News-Letter,* October 15, 1841; Gilbert Osofsky, "Abolitionists, Irish Immigrants, and the Dilemma of Romantic Nationalism," *American Historical Review* 80, no. 4 (1975): 394–98.

29. Garrison and Garrison, *William Lloyd Garrison,* 3:44–45; James Brewer Stewart, *Wendell Phillips: Liberty's Hero* (Baton Rouge: Louisiana State University Press, 1986), 111.

30. *Liberator,* September 8, 1843; Taylor, *British and American Abolitionists,* 172, 194.

31. Riach, "Richard Davis Webb," 165. For recent discussion of the relationship between O'Connell, American abolitionists, and Repealers, see Angela Murphy, "Abolition, Irish Freedom, and Immigrant Citizenship: American Slavery and the Rise and Fall of the American Associations for Irish Repeal" (Ph.D. diss., University of Houston, 2006).

32. Child to Ellis Gray Loring, New York, April 6, 1842, Child Papers, New York Public Library; Lewis Perry, *Childhood, Marriage and Reform: Henry Clarke Wright 1797–1870* (Chicago: University of Chicago Press, 1980), 46.

33. For a discussion of the Free Church controversy, see Rice, *Scots Abolitionists,* 119–40; Blackett, *Building an Antislavery Wall,* 83–87; *Liberator,* May 15, 1846.

34. Taylor, *British and American Abolitionists,* 278, 290.

35. Evangelical Alliance, *Report of the Proceedings of the Conference Held at Freemasons' Hall, London, from August 19th to September 2nd Inclusive, 1846* (London: Patridge and Oakey, 1847), 436–58; *Liberator,* September 25, 1846.

36. *Liberator,* September 11, November 20, 1846.

37. Taylor, *British and American Abolitionists,* 304.

38. Webb to Wright, Dublin, February 22, 1846. English, Irish, Scottish Letters Addressed to Henry C. Wright, 1843–47, Houghton Library, Harvard University; Webb to Chapman, Dublin, July 16, 1846, Anti Slavery Papers.

39. May to J. B. Estlin, Boston, September 26, 1846. Lucretia Mott also called on the leaders of the society to lower the level of their criticism of the BFASS's intentions. See Mott to Chapman, Philadelphia, July 23, 1846. Both in Anti Slavery Papers.

40. Leeds *Times,* n.d., in *Liberator,* February 5, 1847.

41. Taylor, *British and American Abolitionists,* 241.

42. Henry Wigham to Garrison, Edinburgh, July 16, 1850. Anti Slavery Papers.

43. Taylor, *British and American Abolitionists,* 412. His statement on Pennington is quoted in Stacey M. Robertson, *Parker Pillsbury: Radical Abolitionist, Male Feminist* (Ithaca: Cornell University Press, 2000), 107.

44. Robertson, *Parker Pillsbury,* 99–100.

45. Webb to Chapman, Dublin, May 3, 1855, Anti Slavery Papers. Donald Yacavone, *Samuel Joseph May and the Dilemmas of the Liberal Persuasion, 1797–1871* (Philadelphia: Temple University Press, 1991), 166.

46. *Liberator,* June 21, 1861, January 17, 1862; *National Anti Slavery Standard,* September 14, 1861; Samuel May Jr. to Webb, Leicester, February 10, 1863, Webb to Anne Weston, Dublin, December 31, 1861, both in Anti Slavery Papers.

47. *Liberator,* February 7, 1862, April 4, 1862; *National Anti Slavery Standard,* January 25, 1862.

48. Quoted in Riach, "Richard Davis Webb," 156–57.

3

William Lloyd Garrison and Emancipatory Feminism in Nineteenth-Century America

LOIS A. BROWN

As in England, so in this country — the women have done and are doing more for the extirpation of slavery than the other sex. In their petitions to Congress, they outnumber us at least three, perhaps five to one.
— *William Lloyd Garrison, 6 November 1837*

Absorbed as we are in these perilous times, with the great work of unchaining the American bondman, and assisting the hapless and hunted fugitive in his flight from his merciless pursuers to a place of safety, we have little time to consider the inequalities, wrongs, and hardships endured by woman. Our silence, however, must not be set down either to indifference or to a want of independence. In our eyes, the rights of woman and the rights of man are identical — we ask no rights, we advocate no rights for ourselves, which we would not ask and advocate for women.
— *Frederick Douglass, Women's Rights Convention, Worcester, Massachusetts, 1851*

The debut issue of the *Liberator*, the premier American abolitionist newspaper, featured one of the most forceful declarations that William Lloyd Garrison, its visionary editor, ever made. Many are familiar with the poetic pledge in which Garrison laid down the sure foundation on which his politics and his Boston press would rest until America unshackled itself and those enslaved within its borders from the peculiar institution. The well-known passage is suffused with unapologetic self-awareness, precisely articulated outrage, and sheer impatience. "I *will* be as harsh as truth, and as uncompromising as justice. On this subject I do not wish to think, or speak, or write with moderation," insisted Garrison, before delving into thoroughly domestic metaphor to underscore the legitimate urgency of his political convictions and professional intentions. "Tell a man whose house is on fire, to give a moderate alarm; tell him to moderately rescue his wife from the bands of the ravisher; tell the mother to gradually extricate her babe from the fire into which it has fallen," he continued, "but urge not me to use moderation in a case like the present. I am in earnest, — I will not equivocate, — I will not excuse, — I will not retreat a single inch — and I will be heard."[1] These words have come to embody and constitute for many a pithy, forceful, and self-explanatory introduction to Garrison the abolitionist, the journalist, and the man.

This historic and striking proclamation positioned squarely on the front page of the *Liberator* for 1 January 1831 was prefaced by lines that illuminate even further the emancipatory project Garrison was determined to enact. The twenty-six-year-old editor stated plainly that he was "determined to lift up, at every hazard, the standard of emancipation, within sight of Bunker Hill and in the birthplace of liberty. That standard is now unfurled — till every chain be broken and every bondman set free! Let Southern oppressors tremble, — let their secret abettors tremble, — let their Northern apologists, — let all the enemies of the persecuted blacks tremble!" Garrison presented himself in this first issue of the *Liberator* as an indefatigable and earnest standard-bearer. His invocation of Bunker Hill, often regarded as the critical battle of the American Revolution, transformed Garrison at this auspicious professional moment from an avowed pacifist into an impassioned fighter. He appropriated without hesitation a forceful military rhetoric, high patriotic discourse, and cultural ideals of manliness. It was with these weapons that he asserted the intensity of his war on slavery and its attendant corruptions of nation and family.

Garrison's pledge to unfurl the "standard of emancipation" also had substantial implications for antebellum feminism. The army of abolition he commanded was strengthened because it included in its ranks women from diverse racial, religious, class, and labor backgrounds. The abolitionist movement and its institutions benefited substantially from women's work on behalf of the movement. The enterprising constituency of abolitionist women that included the members of the Boston Female Anti-Slavery Society (BFASS), with whom Garrison and his New England colleagues worked extremely closely, developed and implemented some powerful ideas and outreach, and did so to great effect. Garrison did not hesitate to acknowledge their substantial leadership. Writing in 1837 to Elizabeth Pease, a wealthy British Quaker abolitionist after whom he and his wife, Helen, named one of their daughters, Garrison offered sincere praise to lady activists. "As in England, so in this country," he wrote, "the women have done and are doing more for the extirpation of slavery than the other sex. In their petitions to Congress, they outnumber us at least three, perhaps five to one."[2]

The history of women's political activity in America often is linked to the eloquent, but unsuccessful, private petition Abigail Adams made to her husband, the future president John Adams, as he participated in talks at the Continental Congress in 1776. Abigail's overture promised quite directly that there would be an unprecedented mobilization to secure representation and an emphatic rejection of hollow democratic ideals if women's interests were not plainly incorporated into the emerging national discourse. "If particular care and attention are not paid to the ladies," she cautioned in her letter of 31 March 1776 sent from the Adams home in Boston, "we are determined to foment a rebellion and will not hold ourselves bound to obey any laws in which we have no voice or representation."[3] Traditionally, discussions of American women's political activity leap from this independent late eighteenth-century sentiment of Abigail Adams to discussions of the collective abolitionist enterprise in which women figured increasingly more than fifty years later. The absent women's revolutionary narrative is one that scholars continue to consider in their evaluations of women's eighteenth-century political and cultural sensibilities.[4] Indeed, the distance between the eloquent colonial articulation of political interest and the demonstration of antebellum political activity invites a new accounting of the ways in which women — white, native, and those of African descent in America — initiated political action and resistance. It is useful, though, to consider how Adams's remarks illuminate the dynamic connections between women and the political word, and the ways in which the eighteenth- and nineteenth-century political work of women in America was linked deliberately to the power of petition and the manifestation of collective women's resistance in the effort to institutionalize gender equity and freedoms for women.

The transition from Abigail Adams's individual white female advocacy for the rights of women to the broad national and multiracial campaign to abolish slavery in America is significant. If, as the scholar Mark Kann suggests, the "gendering of American politics began with the founders' forgetfulness," then one can appreciate the abolitionists' wisdom in insisting that Americans and the world remember, in every possible context, the invalidated rights and imposed suffering of the enslaved individuals in their midst.[5] The abolitionist women who shaped, financed, and invigorated the movement to free the millions enslaved in America proved themselves the rightful heirs of Adams, even as they tempered the rebellion of which she spoke and distanced themselves from the conscientious lawlessness she sanctioned. The process of petitioning, itself an act of eloquent political advocacy, depended on clear, persuasive articulations of the issues at hand, facilitated intimate encounters rather than impersonal public suasion, benefited from the activists' social mobility, and was linked clearly to the intensified women's abolitionist campaigns that held elected officials accountable to national ideals and religious standards. As the historian Susan Zaeske has observed, women's antislavery work was inextricably linked to antislavery petitioning, activities that began insistently in the early 1830s and ceased in 1865 at the end of the American Civil War. These public documents, sophisticated for their political acuity and remarkable for their invocations of women's piety and domesticity, ultimately bore the signatures of some three million women. Such a stunning collection of signatures constitutes a mighty body of political will, one made manifest as antislavery petitioners from Vermont to Ohio moved "door to door" through their cities, towns, and villages.[6]

Abolitionist feminist politics and strategies of engagement would figure prominently in Garrison's decades-long battle to eradicate slavery. The rhetoric and collective project of emancipation, especially as Garrison articulated it, was wholly evocative for many who ascribed to it. Abolitionist work catapulted many women who were committed to national ideals, social justice, and reform to leadership positions in interracial organizations, and it also accorded some of them unprecedented visibility in predominantly male institutional groups such as the New England Slavery Society. Abolitionism quickly became linked to feminist ambitions, and its evolution as a highly gendered enterprise would last well beyond the end of the Civil War. "This is a struggle for her redemption," wrote Garrison in spring 1836 in a letter to Helen as he referenced the potential power of women's work for the movement.[7]

Garrison brought his legendary zeal to bear on his feminist abolitionist projects, efforts that were primarily abolitionist in goal and decidedly gendered in operation. For such convictions, he garnered the respect of formidable women like Elizabeth Cady Stanton, a forthright women's rights activist who appreciated his "noble views" of women.[8] Garrison and his female colleagues negotiated complex public and private perspectives on race, sex, and nation as they integrated antislavery organizations, established an impressive network of female antislavery societies, provided vital funding support, and sustained the men who depended on them as husbands and kin. As the historian and Garrison biographer Henry Mayer notes, "When cautious souls challenged the participation of women in the abolitionist movement as improper and unnecessarily provocative, Garrison leaped to the defense of women's rights."⁹ Garrison offered vital rhetorical and political support to female antislavery societies, cultivated women abolitionists, protested antislavery institutional discrimination by and against women, and championed freeborn, self-emancipated, and formerly enslaved women. His broad application of abolitionist principles enabled him to play an integral part in the evolution of the feminist abolitionist movement. He also influenced and was affected substantially by antebellum applications of emancipatory feminism by women determined to achieve the abolition of slavery and the freedom of American women.

William Lloyd Garrison's founding of the *Liberator* coincided with the broad institutionalization of antebellum female abolition. Women abolitionists in the 1830s joined a rapidly growing network of antislavery societies that ranged from regional heavyweights like the New England Anti-Slavery Society founded in Boston to smaller town enterprises such as Ohio's Ashtabula County Female Antislavery Society, founded in 1835 in a Lake Erie region dotted with Underground Railroad safe houses. Historians suggest that by the late 1830s, when there were more than two million slaves in the nation, some one hundred thousand individuals were affiliated with the more than 1,000 state and local antislavery organizations established throughout the northern and midwestern states.¹⁰ The historian Julie Roy Jeffrey and others have confirmed that women found the cause appealing and often responded deliberately to the calls to action. Nearly 25 percent, or 41 of the 183 antislavery societies that existed in Massachusetts in 1838, were female societies. In addition to these ladies' organizations, there were more than a dozen juvenile antislavery societies thriving right alongside them.¹¹

Garrison's central feminist projects, many of which had decidedly northern and New England contexts, also were linked explicitly and implicitly to race matters. He worked closely with women of color to integrate abolitionist organizations in terms of both gender and race; he also was a renegade in his support of African American women's political autonomy, and he used his influence and connections to finance timely and unexpected interventions that exposed the problematic limits of abolitionist rhetoric and practice. Garrison promoted the leadership potential of women of both races, and he was known for being inclined to catapult some into positions of public scrutiny without giving them full warning or gaining their approval. He made such dramatic moves because he was a savvy propagandist, but also because he appreciated the substantial impact that women's experiences, beliefs, and work could have on public opinion, political issues, and the rehabilitation of nineteenth-century American culture.

"Where there is a human being," declared William Lloyd Garrison, " I see God-given rights inherent in that being, whatever may be the sex or complexion."[12] This matter-of-fact emphasis on humanity and the crisp insistence on the marriage of humanity and equality mark indelibly Garrison's life and politics. Such sentiments also hint at the thinking that resulted in Garrison's unapologetic effort to propel women out of the private sphere of moral influence and onto the public stage of nineteenth-century reform. It was not always this clear for Garrison, though. His early thoughts about the useful contributions of women were conservative and consistent with traditional perspectives on the appropriate roles of nineteenth-century women.

Garrison initially espoused a rather conventional view of how women could contribute to the political causes of the day. In the early 1830s, for example, he had not considered truly the potential scope of female antislavery activism. Yet, even as he worked his way toward a bold conception of women's political potential, Garrison published works that began the powerful abolitionist work of emotional suasion. Articles published in the *Liberator,* especially those by women of color identified only by first names, pseudonyms, or the respectful phrase "a lady of color," reinforced Garrison's traditionalist views and used accounts of female slave experience to elicit moral and political outrage. A piece entitled "Sorrows of A Female Heart," for instance, focused on the awful plight of enslaved women, individuals "torn from the side of affection" and forced to bid "final adieu" to friends, family, husbands, and "her helpless offspring." Attributed to Charlotte, "a young lady of color," the concise paragraph addressed directly the "female heart" on which Garrison also focused in his early abolitionist outreach. "Lift up your eyes and look upon the world, and let the surrounding scenes affect your hearts," encouraged the author before offering a direct plea to the *Liberator*'s lady readers: "Female reader, will you not fall upon your knees, and lift up your voices to heaven for those who are in bondage? For life appears to them like a lingering death, clouded with wo and hung round with despair, where peace and comfort have expired."[13] The publication of such sentiments, which increased significantly when Garrison early on made changes to the size, layout, and format of the *Liberator,* also reflected Garrison's own growing emotional commitment to the cause. In 1836, the *Glasgow Chronicle* reported Garrison's response to the birth of his son George Thompson Garrison and supposedly quoted the editor directly from a letter that as yet has not been unearthed. Garrison was credited as having said that "the news of his birth gives great pleasure to my abolition friends" and also offering the following illuminating reflection: "Methinks my hatred of slavery was feeble before I had a wife and child; but as the ties of life increase, I felt my abhorrence of the impious system constantly augmenting."[14]

As many Garrison historians have observed, his perspective on the woman question came to be explicitly political and linked quite directly to the public sphere. Mayer notes, for example, that "for Garrison the woman question clearly demonstrated how the logic of reform united all good causes and carried them to radical new ground."[15] Considerations of the woman question involved heated discussions about the political disenfranchisement of the ladies, the educational segregation and limited formal and public intellectual opportunities available, the professional containment of women, and their highly regulated social experiences. Such debates were enlivened by the use of such terms as *bondage, slave, master,* and *freedom,* words that pertained specifically to the enslavement of Africans and others but that became evocative metaphors for the plight of women.

In his interactions with women in the abolitionist sphere, Garrison also confronted some striking tendencies and problematic divides. He witnessed firsthand their deployment of metaphoric abolition. This application of powerful rhetoric and ideology was achieved when activist women applied key slavery and abolitionist terms and imagery not solely to the essentially homeless African American masses, but also to the seemingly homebound population of white women, individuals confined to domestic spheres governed by ironclad genteel codes of virtue, piety, and domesticity. White abolitionist women in particular gained insights into their own subjugation as they joined the abolitionist effort and studied the bondage of Africans in America. Their political consciousness evolved in direct relation to the plight of enslaved women; many activists were convinced, as the historian Stacey Robertson notes, that "woman's sensitive moral nature and sisterly connection to female slaves created in them a special obligation to help free those in bondage."[16] In no time, though, the discourse of slavery became integral to the discourse of woman's liberation. "In striving to strike [the slave's] irons off, we found most surely that we were manacled ourselves," announced Abby Kelley in 1838. The Worcester, Massachusetts, activist was determined to share publicly the antislavery message, and for doing so she suffered considerable harassment and was slandered as a loose woman.[17] Charges such as these were typical of the slurs used to suggest the impurity of women's political work and to undermine their status and self-confidence as able activists. Ernestine Susmond Rose, a Polish-born pioneer in the American women's rights movement, also spoke to this untenable categorization of women as well. Rose's protest was fueled by her compelling experiences of patriarchal will during her teenage years. As an adolescent, she had spiritedly rejected the efforts of her father, a rabbi, to marry her off as a way to silence what he deemed her anti-Jewish heresies, and, even more remarkable, she prevailed in her self-defense against the spurned suitor, who brought suit against her for damages. Rose, who was instrumental to the passage in New

York in 1848 of the nation's first property law for married women, minced no words when she forcefully declared, "Woman is a slave, from the cradle to the grave. Father, guardian, husband — master still. One conveys her, like a piece of property, over to the other."[18]

Rose's searing observation resonated with the late eighteenth-century claims the British feminist and philosopher Mary Wollstonecraft and others made when they first linked the discourse of slavery to that of marriage. Eric Foner notes that Wollstonecraft and her peers made this rich rhetorical connection because they believed that "true equality was impossible until the institution of marriage had been fundamentally transformed."[19] As the historian Louise Newman and others have observed, white abolitionist women "emphasized the similarities between their own oppressed status as wives and daughters under patriarchy and the debased condition of 'the Negro' under slavery."[20] In so doing, they sparred with proponents of antifeminist discourse, the thinking that enabled writers for the *New York Herald* to ask in 1852, "How did woman first become subject to man?" and then to conclude in the same breath that "by her nature, her sex, just as the negro is and always will be, to the end, inferior to the white race, and, therefore doomed to subjection."[21]

Powerful and relevant as it was, this "idiom of freedom and unfreedom," as Foner describes it, had the potential to diminish or, to be less pessimistic, to distract the work of white women abolitionists in Garrison's New England circles. As Foner also observes in his consideration of freedom in the age of emancipation, "The slavery of sex became an all-encompassing critique of the subordination of women, and the female slave an emblem for the condition of all women."[22] The historian Amy Dru Stanley concurs, noting, "Since its inception, the woman movement had underscored the legal symmetry between slavery and marriage, deploring the wife's lack of personal and property rights and calling for statutory reform of the common law rules of coverture."[23] This emphasis was a significant "misinterpretation," according to the scholar Jean Fagan Yellin, who argues that "the free women misinterpreted the situation of slave women, and . . . they misinterpreted their own: they were not, after all, literally in irons." Yellin continues, noting that white women's "appropriation of the emblems of antislavery discourse masked the very real differences between the oppression of black slave women and free white women in America — and the very real differences in the character of the struggle against these oppressions."[24]

Opportunities did exist for white abolitionist women to make vital political observations and to reconsider nineteenth-century feminist ideology. In Boston, a principal stop on the Underground Railroad and a city in which there were high numbers of self-emancipated and formerly enslaved women, it was possible for whites to see the embodiment of the theories they were cultivating. Boston also was home to a defined freeborn community of color, one in which the success of African American teachers, ministers, and printers, doctresses, and classical singers complicated the binary oppositions on which white women's domestic abolitionist outrage depended. One of the most important interventions Garrison would make had everything to do with countering the subversive seduction of racial essentialism and the perspectives it accommodated. The work of abolition could be the special province of Bostonians and Garrisonians. It also should be, Garrison argued, a multiracial, socially diverse enterprise, one that did not relegate the African American subject to that of metaphoric embodiment of white women's domestic distress. Avoiding this problematic categorization was key, as Yellin observes, because failing to do so transformed the core ideals of feminist abolitionist practice and had devastating effects on women of color within the movement. The "discourse of antislavery feminism became not liberating but confining," asserts Yellin, "when it colored the self-liberated Woman and Sister white and reassigned the role of the passive victim, which the patriarchy traditionally had reserved for white women, to women who were black."[25] Garrison also was striving to prevent whites from luxuriating in or depending upon the notion that people of color, and in particular women of color, were always and already subject to change and not the agents of it.

Women of color engaged in formal abolitionist work in order to accomplish specific political, racial, cultural, and democratic goals. Abolitionism certainly was a means by which they could establish and assert the new and uplifting models of American womanhood. This activism enabled women of color to actively preserve their tenuous hold on freedom. Indeed, free African American women sometimes were compelled to take up this bold work when they realized that in truth, despite their residencies in the North or established reputations, their hold on freedom and family could be completely undone. Sarah Douglass of Philadelphia, an influential African American Quaker educator and cofounder of the Philadelphia Anti-Slavery Society, was jarred into abolitionist activism by the sight of a slave catcher. Douglass's account of her activist epiphany, published in the *Liberator*, revealed the luxuries of freedom and the power of bondage. "I had formed a little world of my own," she confessed, "and [I] cared not to move beyond its precincts. But how was the scene changed when I beheld the oppressor lurking on the border of my own peaceful home! I saw his iron hand stretched forth to seize me as his prey, and the cause of the slave became my own." She recalled that she "started up and with one mighty effort threw from me the lethargy which had covered me as a mantle for years; and determined, by the help of the Almighty, to use the exertion in my power to elevate the character of my wronged and neglected race."[26] Douglass was like one resurrected from the dead at this formative moment of realization and accountability. Such awakenings continued to occur for freeborn women of color and for those whose family histories of colonial-era enslavement had become part of an increasingly distant past.

Abolitionist women like Douglass found that their activism and interventionist work often enabled them to sidestep or even disregard traditional gender and racial expectations. However, the cultural emancipation for which they were working did not obscure the primary goal of abolition. As Yellin has stated, the historical and written records of African American women's activism, and in particular the efforts of formerly enslaved women, reveal that these women "did not, however, confuse the experience of free women with their experience as female slaves. Nor did they confuse the free woman's struggle for self liberation from a metaphorical slavery with their own struggle for self liberation from slavery."[27] This clarity of purpose was an essential element of successful feminist abolitionism. Indeed, abolitionist women of color with whom Garrison worked closely recognized the importance of these distinctions. They were wary of the all-too-easy acts of essentialization that dissolved the realities and complexities of race and gender and overlooked wholly diverse family histories of freedom or of servitude. While such lapses certainly had the potential to hobble the movement, they also had the potential to educate Americans and thus contribute to a more deliberately democratic and just postslavery American world.

The work that white women undertook on behalf of the shackled African masses was inspired by gender solidarity and informed by racial difference. Yet, it quickly became work informed by racialized gender realities and by the larger universal history of women. Scholars have documented well the ways in which antislavery work served as a vehicle by which many leaders and members of the abolitionist women's movement sought to achieve their own self-emancipation. It was a predictable transition, though, precisely because the most evocative image was that of the enslaved woman. It was the "presence," of this figure, writes Yellin, which "jolted free women, forcing them to examine the condition of slaves in relation to their own situation."[28] Sobering accounts of the mistreatment of female slaves were effective recruitment tools and conjured up for audiences and prospective antislavery society members powerful and "special imaginative and sympathetic connection[s] with the female slave."[29] The pioneering antislavery lecturer and future physician Sarah Parker Remond, a Salem, Massachusetts, native and the daughter of the prosperous Curaçao-born caterer John Parker Remond and his wife, Nancy, spoke to great effect about the plight of enslaved women during her late antebellum-era speaking tour in England. Her illustrations underscored the vexed ways in which whiteness could offer little protection to women in bondage: "What is slavery? who can tell?" Remond was reported to have asked in "deep and thrilling tones" as she delivered a ninety-minute speech before a standing-room-only audience in the Music Hall of Warrington, England, on 24 January 1859. She continued, "In the open market place women are exposed for sale — their persons not always covered. Yes, I can tell you English men and women, that women are sold into slavery with cheeks like the lily and the rose, as well as those that might compare with the wing of the raven. They are exposed for sale, and subjected to the most shameful indignities. The more Anglo-Saxon blood that mingles with the blood of the slave, the more gold is poured out when the auctioneer has a woman for sale, because they are sold to be concubines for white Americans. They are not sold for plantation slaves."[30] Remond's revelations certainly were calculated to create indignation. Her commentary was designed to underscore, first, a universal desire to protect female virtue and modesty, and then to encourage listeners to bold action and collective work to achieve racial freedom and equality. The call to abolitionist work that Remond issued deftly colored anew the bodies rendered vulnerable by slavery. She whitened the black female slave body that audiences expected to behold and in so doing, she created a new call for emancipatory activism, one fueled by individual outrage that indulged in and was rooted in, both subtly and explicitly, caste consciousness.

The original work of emancipatory feminism saw women like the southern abolitionist Angelina Grimké and the New Englanders Susan Paul, Abby Kelley Foster, and Remond claiming unprecedented public and political spheres of influence. Yet, this vital work became an increasingly contested and racialized field fraught with tensions when white women's thoroughly gendered desire for suffrage, marriage and family rights, and other social and political reforms were privileged over more immediate racial and expansive gender-inclusive goals. White American women transposed their frustration about their disenfranchisement as wives, workers, and dependents into the antislavery campaign. Stanley has observed quite pointedly that "feminists claimed that marriage belonged at the very center of public debate over the outcome of slave emancipation."[31] Indeed, Elizabeth Cady Stanton, the chief proponent of women's suffrage and wife of the active abolitionist Henry Stanton, advocated this belief more than a decade before slavery was abolished. "The rights of humanity are more grossly betrayed at the altar than at the auction block of the slave-holder," she declared in 1851 in a passionate letter to her cousin, the bold humanitarian and philanthropist Gerrit Smith.[32] Ideas like those Stanton held, however, were countered by other perspectives, ones that underscored the primary and enduring importance of gender solidarity in the fight against slavery. Such sentiments, which kept race slavery rather than female bondage in focus, were eloquently expressed throughout the antebellum period. In the early 1830s, for example, a member of an Ohio female antislavery society insisted plainly that " 'we should be less women if the nameless wrongs of . . . the slaves of our sex . . . did not fill us with horror' and awaken 'a deep personal interest in this matter.' "[33] In the early postbellum period, the women's rights reformer Lucy Stone and the abolitionist Abby Kelley Foster debated the priorities. Stone, who was the first American woman to earn a college degree when she graduated from Oberlin College in 1847 and famously retained her maiden name when she married, insisted that Kelley's interest in African American rights rather than women's suffrage was the result of a "strange blindness," a condition that made her "prefe[r] the poor half loaf of justice for the Negro to the grand principles of equal rights and universal suffrage." Kelley countered matter-of-factly and told her longtime colleague, "I should look on myself as a monster of selfishness if, while I see my neighbor's daughter held and treated like a beast—as thousands still are all over the rural districts of the south . . . I would turn from helping them to secure to my daughter political equality."[34] Exchanges like these reinforce the reality described by scholars like Robert Riegel, who notes that at critical times, such as the onset of the Civil War, women like Stanton and others rallied their individual and institutional powers, "used their energies to support the war," channeled their efforts through such established groups as the Women's National Loyal League, and did so "since they had all been abolitionists before they had been feminists."[35]

Abolitionist work influenced greatly strategies for white female advancement in the antebellum and postbellum eras. The perspective on real and metaphorical bondage that Stanton had, for example, was shaped by her participation in American and international antislavery circles. She concluded early on in her increasingly public political life that "slavery is a political question, created and sustained by law and must be put down by law." She articulated her thinking in a way that hints heavily at an abstracted regard for slavery rather than an intensely personalized ideology against it. In doing so, however, she may have freed herself and others who approached the issues similarly to work for suffrage and woman's cultural emancipation. Such perspectives and identified high stakes also contributed to the increasingly costly allegiance to the advancement of white women, whom she regarded as shackled by patriarchal practice. Members of the women's suffrage and rights movement, which never was divorced fully from the abolitionist movement, confronted intensifying conflicts with those who sought to achieve equality for

African American women and men before tending to the universal plight of women.

Feminist and abolitionist investments in the plight of the slave would shift dramatically in the early post–Civil War years. This development was in stark contrast to the rallying efforts made by many women activists as the war began. According to the historian Ellen DuBois, "Women's rights activists subordinated all other interests to the fate of slavery, and suspended feminist activity for the length of the war."[36] At crucial Civil War moments, such as the institution of the Emancipation Proclamation in January 1863, women of the National Loyal Women's League followed the lead of Stanton and Susan B. Anthony and "push[ed] for a constitutional amendment abolishing slavery." Leading political figures such as Senator Charles Sumner of Massachusetts appreciated greatly such boldness; he "credited their work on collecting four hundred thousand signatures on petitions with much of the impetus behind the Thirteenth Amendment."[37] It was this very passage of amendments granting rights of citizenship to African Americans and suffrage to men of the race, however, that derailed the long-standing and convenient arguments about shared bondage. "Antebellum suffrage ideology often emphasized a common victimhood," writes Newman, and, in contrast, "postbellum suffrage ideology stressed white women's racial-cultural superiority to newly enfranchised male constituencies — not just black men, but also naturalized immigrant men."[38] This was at times a ferocious shift, one that revealed at key moments the inherent racial divide and tensions within the larger American women's movement. At the National Woman Suffrage Convention held in Washington, D.C., in January 1869, Stanton delivered an address that was tinged with xenophobic ire. She called her fellow members to action by urging them to "think of Patrick and Sambo and Hans and Yung Tung who do not know the difference between a monarchy and a republic, who can not read the Declaration of Independence or Webster's spelling-book, making laws for Lucretia Mott, Ernestine L. Rose and Anna E. Dickinson."[39] The references to Irish, African, German, and Asian men is one thing to consider here; another is the fact that Stanton's list of victimized women for all intents and purposes is completely anglicized: she refers to Mott, her fellow co-organizer of the Seneca Falls convention of 1848, Rose, a Polish immigrant, the wife of an Englishman, and a successful ethnic Euro-American who was one of the first women to speak publicly in America, and Dickinson, a Quaker who in 1864 became the first woman ever to address the Congress. It is telling that Stanton's outrage did not prompt her, for example, to underscore the multiracial reality of women's disenfranchisement so clearly illustrated by the documented experiences of Maria Stewart, Sojourner Truth, Sarah Remond, and Harriet Jacobs.

When considered in the context of nineteenth-century white women's political activism, emancipatory feminism, especially that which was articulated and practiced in the antebellum period, reflects a collective desire to undo the corset created by the cult of true womanhood and legalized subjugation and to don instead garb that was more accommodating of white women's strides toward full citizenship rights, suffrage, ownership of property, rights to their own wages, protection from domestic abuse, and equal education. Garrison, the stalwart dean of abolition, believed strongly, though, that such work should not eclipse the original and primary objectives of the abolition he espoused. He sought to remind his female colleagues that there was an original, urgent, and pressing emancipation to be achieved. But even as he urged attention to the slavery issue, Garrison recognized the enormous benefits his movement could elicit from women — and secondarily from upstanding men — by consistently interpreting aspects of chattel slavery in the recognizable and accepted language of high domesticity. Thus, Garrison was able to acknowledge white women's protests of marital and social inequality even as he insisted emphatically that such outrage could not be divorced from or supercede the injustices imposed upon silenced women of color. African American women, he argued, were denied the protection and privilege of marriage, but in addition their elementary virtue and basic physical safety perpetually were under siege. Writing in the *Liberator* in 1832, he declared, "We wish to rescue from infamy a million female slaves" and, in characteristic style, spoke on behalf of the collective abolitionist masses when he intoned, "We shall not cease from our efforts." He did not flinch in the face of sexual facts as he railed against the gradualists and calumniators whom he regarded as "the friends and abettors" of proslavery advocates who tolerated illicit, violent, and devastating amalgamation. On this occasion, Garrison applied high domestic codes to slavery, suggesting that "illicit intercourse" was reason enough that the system should be abolished immediately. "We are for breaking up the slave system at once," he declared, "and thus prevent this intercourse. Our traducers say, No; let slavery alone — let the tide of pollution continue to swell — and let the female slaves have no protection for their virtue, so that they may be violated always, as at present, with impunity."[40]

African American women with whom Garrison corresponded and associated at antislavery meetings and whom he published in the *Liberator* were both freeborn and formerly enslaved. They too brought additional agendas to their work for abolition. In Boston, women like Harriet Hayden, Anne Catherine Paul, and Nancy Gardiner were members of ambitious families and also were involved in collective initiatives designed to reveal and support the political acumen, financial savvy, gentility, and intellectual power of their community. These women also were deliberate in their appropriation of key cultural terms that placed their abolitionist work in a larger context of African American freedoms. White women looked to African experience as they appropriated to great dramatic effect the rhetoric of bondage and chattel slavery; women of color invoked highly racialized white social discourse in their effort to achieve true freedom in America. Emancipatory feminism for women of color was born of their inherited fight against proscription and prejudice as well as of their marginalization in the high-stakes battles fought over true womanhood.

Women like those who in 1833 revived the Colored Female Religious and Moral Society of Salem, Massachusetts, some fifteen years after its founding, regarded their efforts to institutionalize and racialize propriety and decorum as part of a feminist project that would confer tangible liberties upon women living free in the North. This deliberate racialized effort to assert true black womanhood complemented and even shaped their antislavery work as well. In addition to establishing effective female antislavery groups such as the Salem Female Anti-Slavery Society, which the gifted Philadelphia-born Charlotte Forten and Remond helped to found in 1834, African American women systematically and routinely created moral, intellectual, and uplift societies. Mercy Morris, Sally Coleman, Betsey Blanchard, and others were members of a Salem, Massachusetts, society that Garrison hailed for the "cheering evidences of [its] appreciation of virtue and knowledge." The society's constitution, which the ladies carefully composed, included several purposeful articles, one of which declared that all members would "resolve to be charitably watchful over each other; to advise, caution and admonish where we judge there is occasion, and that it may be useful; and we promise not to resent, but kindly and thankfully receive such friendly advice or reproof from any one of our members." The adoption of such principles underscored the high regard for individual and collective uplift. When these tenets were linked to racial abolition, they helped to reinforce the rightful place in the movement for women of color. These principles also gave to free women of color invaluable social protection in the predominantly white, patriarchal institutional abolitionist and antislavery movements.

The phrase *emancipatory feminism* resonated keenly with women like those of the Salem Religious and Moral Society and with Bostonians such as Susan Paul. Paul, a second-generation freeborn woman of color and a schoolteacher, was the daughter of Catherine Waterhouse, an enterprising and beloved educator from Cambridge, and her husband, Thomas, a learned minister, freeborn son of an enslaved French and Indian War veteran, and a native of Exeter, New Hampshire. The Reverend Thomas Paul was appointed the first minister of Boston's first African American Baptist Church, and shortly after the Boston church was established in 1806 he traveled to New York City, where he was instrumental in the founding of the Abyssinian Baptist Church. Paul also was a missionary to Haiti in the early 1800s. His brother Nathaniel, also a Baptist minister, later settled in Albany, New York. Nathaniel Paul was a close colleague of Garrison's, and the two men spent an extraordinary summer together in the early 1830s touring England and raising money for the abolitionist cause and for the Canadian Negro settlement community that Paul represented. Susan Paul worked closely with Garrison on private and public matters. He offered practical help to her and the family following the death of her grandparents and her father in the early 1830s, promoted her as a visionary African American historian and educator, and strategized with her on how best to break down the useless racial obstructions that compromised the Boston women's abolitionist circle.

The early female antislavery societies like those in Boston — of which Susan Paul and Julia Williams, a member of both Boston's African American community and the integrated BFASS, became a part — could not sidestep race. Racial realities manifested themselves in myriad ways, ranging from seating arrangements at abolitionist and church meetings to the inspired interracial pairings in October 1835 when BFASS members walked arm in arm in white and African American pairs as they exited the building that a mob was moments away from storming. Race matters also emerged as unwieldy realities linked to the politics of intermarriage and the glaring savageries of concubinage. The articulated missions that appeared in constitutions meant that members not only might well have to separate sobering racial facts from divisive racial fictions, but make it a priority to do so. It was at this critical moral and political juncture in women's abolitionist thinking and practice that Garrison sought to plant that "standard of emancipation" to which he referred in the first issue of the *Liberator*. The South was not the only place where chains, bondmen and -women, and oppressors existed. Garrison was committed to the meaningful liberation of the lady soldiers who regarded themselves as members of the great army of abolition.

As the auction block was to slavery, the *Liberator* was to emancipatory feminism. Garrison transformed it into a highly public stage upon which women like the Bostonian Maria Stewart, the gifted and thoroughly tested orphan, could deliver their urgent calls for racial uplift and high moral integrity and their indictments of emotional and political sloth, spiritual apathy, and unforgivable civic acquiescence. It was the platform upon which a daughter of southern slaveholders like Angelina Grimké could be placed and from which she could reveal herself as one unafraid of martyrdom for the cause of emancipation.

Considerations of Garrison and the politics of nineteenth-century feminist work are thoroughly intertwined with the public political work Garrison conducted in the *Liberator*. Both proceeded, often unpredictably, in public forums such as convention meetings and abolitionist rallies. Garrison used the *Liberator* as the primary vehicle of his advocacy for and negotiations with women, his vehement and demure, privileged and impoverished, bold and sometimes reticent fellow abolitionists. The *Liberator* grew quickly to include weekly reports about the activities of female antislavery societies as well as reviews of the lectures they arranged and the new publications that members produced. The Ladies' Department in the paper was a powerful extension of the *Liberator*'s articles; it routinely published copies of female antislavery society constitutions and reprinted wrenching political poetry such as the 1833 work entitled "The Colored Mother of New England" that appeared in the *Weekly Recorder*. A representative sample of the Ladies' Department included engaging didactic materials, sets of essays produced by African American female organizations such as the 1832 treatises composed by members of the "Society of colored ladies in Providence who have associated for mutual improvement in literature and morals," and some of the earliest works of African American writing.[41]

The *Liberator* stage was an expensive realm, however, and certain women occupied that space at great cost and personal sacrifice. Both Stewart and Grimké, for example, experienced significant and potentially disorienting alienation from kin and native community as a direct result of their professional and political relationships with Garrison. Others, like the enterprising abolitionist and temperance worker Susan Paul, managed and resisted Garrison's enthusiastic and unapologetic tugs and jolts; she was especially vigilant about regulating his manipulation of her politics and took great pains to maintain a steady hand on the evolution of her political consciousness and public persona.

Stewart, one of the most memorable women to explode the notion of emancipatory feminism, was the first woman in America to address an audience of men and women, or, as it was called then, "a profane audience." The *Liberator* was key both to Stewart's emancipation as a progressive intellectual and to her condemnation as an outspoken woman. Garrison published her fiery writings and speeches, and it was in his newspaper that she made her political and writerly debut. In 1831, her essay "Religion and the Pure Principles of Morality, The Sure Foundation on Which We Must Build" launched what would be a brilliant, hotly contested, and short-lived public career in Boston. Garrison's patronage of Stewart enabled him to secure yet another political, historical, and racial triumph for the *Liberator*. Stewart's essay, the first published African American woman's political manifesto, confirmed her as the pioneering American woman public political speaker of her day. It was a vital piece, one in which Stewart spurred on her African American community to develop its talents and in which she insisted that the United States honor the noble aims of the Constitution and "provide all people with the universal birth right of justice and freedom."

One of the invaluable aspects of the controversial piece that ultimately contributed to Stewart's exile from Boston is that it reveals the sincere political camaraderie between Garrison and Stewart. Stewart urged her readers to "encourage the noble-hearted Garrison" and in so doing reconfirmed her solidarity with the African Americans who provided the vital seed money and subscriptions that financed the *Liberator* in its first years. Stewart also demonstrated her firm hold on emancipatory feminism, asserting to all that her affiliation with Garrison did not produce her work or compromise the independence of her thoughts: "It is God alone that has inspired my heart to feel for Afric's woes," she declared in the essay, which exhorted her readers to "fret not yourselves because of evil doers."

Garrison's support, mentorship, and political investment in Stewart did not end with the publication of her important and historic lecture. The *Liberator* later published notices of Stewart's upcoming public addresses before such groups as the Afric-American Female Intelligence Society and in such venues as the African Masonic Hall, the Franklin Hall in downtown Boston, and the African Baptist Church, a jewel on Beacon Hill that stands adjacent to the Abiel Smith School, the nation's first public building dedicated to the education of African American children.

Stewart's achievements were remarkable in many ways, and especially because she was an independent speaker, a woman who did not depend on or claim traditional institutional memberships or contexts as she disseminated her messages, made bold assessments of women's potential, and dispensed unapologetic and forthright prescriptions for racial uplift. Ultimately, Stewart's candor, her readily apparent political autonomy, and her social independence frustrated Boston's African American and white patriarchy. Frustrated but not silenced, Stewart chose to end her public political career in Boston and relocate to other northern ground that she hoped would be more fertile. Before she left for New York City, though, she redirected the political capital she had acquired and the activist momentum she and Garrison had generated. Stewart essentially knighted another Bostonian, Susan Paul, to carry the standard of high expectations and daring activism she and Garrison had protected.

The emancipatory feminist project Garrison began with Stewart evolved considerably as he began to work with Paul. She was a daughter of Boston's revered African American institutions, and her family was at the helm of the impressive founding group of African Americans who established and maintained the African Baptist Church. Paul's energetic work at a downtown Boston public school helped to integrate the mass of Boston's public school teachers. In addition, she was a founding member of African American temperance societies and a gifted singer who regularly performed at stirring classical concerts staged on Beacon Hill. She recognized that one could multiply one's political capital by investing it in institutional organizations such as the New England Anti-Slavery Society (NEASS), the group her father, Thomas, enabled when he granted Garrison and his band of abolitionist brothers a meeting room in the African Baptist Church in December 1833. With Paul, Garrison was able to refine and deepen his understanding of the constantly broadening and intensifying "woman question"; he also was able to experiment with his expanding institutional power as the recognized and formidable leader of the nation's premier abolitionist organizations and publications.

Paul's deft handling of New England's sober gender politics and her incursions on NEASS's practices stand as inspired examples of the emancipatory feminism that appealed so deeply to Garrison. The NEASS was one of the more welcoming antislavery groups; African Americans and white women were able to attend and to participate in its gatherings and conventions. There remained, though, pockets that had no interest in seeing women take on visible roles. In 1841, ironically, the year in which Paul's promising life was cut tragically short by tuberculosis, the organization endeavored to address the "general question of women's rights." As one member recalled later, the group "turned to the constitution of our society. We there found that all persons, who were members of the society, had equal rights in its meetings. Unless, therefore, we were prepared to vote that women are not *persons,* we could not deny them the common privileges of membership." The society concluded that "the original ground of this society, the first in the United States, was, that every person should be left free to advance the cause of the slave in such a manner as should be approved by his own conscience. . . . People of all sects, all colors, and both sexes, are free to work for the slave, as seems to them best." Ultimately, the NEASS imposed the burden of acceptance on its members: "The only question this association asks, or according to its own principles has a right to ask, is whether its members believe immediate, unconditional emancipation to be a duty, and are willing to labor for its advancement."[42]

Discussion of Garrison and women's advancement often becomes a narrative about his particular personal commitments and about private interactions with women that had thoroughly public ramifications. Susan Paul was a twenty-four-year-old teacher in one of Boston's segregated primary schools when she made her formal debut as an abolitionist on 14 September 1833. Paul's debut as a public abolitionist occurred less than two weeks after Stewart's explosive public speaking career in Boston came to an end. In what amounted to a bold act of feminist intervention that reconfirmed Stewart's capacity for unconventional and visionary politics, Stewart enthusiastically "endorsed the work that Susan Paul was poised to begin within the protected sphere of white abolition."[43] Stewart attempted to prepare Bostonians, many of whom gathered in the African Baptist Church, where Thomas Paul presided over Stewart's marriage, for the intriguing changes ahead. In a prophecy that quickly would be made manifest, Stewart urged her colleagues to "be no longer astonished that God at this eventful period should raise up your own females to strive by their example both in public and private, to assist those who are endeavoring to stop the strong current of prejudice that flows so profusely against us at present."[44]

Paul did not let Stewart's clarion call go unheard; yet she recognized the need to make careful alliances as she embarked upon innovative activism that signaled her own political liberation as well as her emancipation from certain cultural codes pertaining to true womanhood. Paul prepared the ground of abolition carefully in order to protect not just her own reputation but that of her family as well and to secure her promising political agenda. Paul's first move was to create a formal partnership with Garrison and the NEASS. Paul became the first African American woman to take out a life membership in the organization, which described itself as one whose members would "endeavor, by all means sanctioned by law, humanity and religion, to effect the abolition of slavery, to improve the character and condition of the free people of color, to inform and correct public opinion in relation to their situation and rights, and obtain for them equal civil and political rights and privileges with the whites."[45] One of Paul's earliest fellow female members was Prudence Crandall, the enterprising Connecticut schoolteacher who suffered greatly when she integrated her female academy and thus protested the divisive segregation and racial oppression that plagued New England. In August 1833, when she joined NEASS, Paul became one of the society's three African American members.[46] Her sizeable fifteen-dollar subscription was part of a calculated effort to ensure her success as a public abolitionist and to protect her because she was an activist woman. Barely four weeks after she became officially affiliated with the NEASS, Paul escorted a group of her students into an NEASS convention meeting. Her charges were members of the Juvenile Choir, which she had founded, and were as young as three and as old as twelve years of age.

The choir delivered several selections appropriate to the abolitionist enterprise and were a complete success. They became featured participants at NEASS meetings and were soon not only accepting invitations to perform at regional antislavery society rallies but also staging their own community concerts. In the spring of 1834, they performed at an NEASS meeting that saw the meeting's "spacious hall . . . crowded to excess, and hundreds went away who were utterly unable to gain admission."[47] One attendee exclaimed that the "tuneful performances of the juvenile choir elicited the strongest expressions of heart-felt admiration, and must have softened the prejudice of many a listener."[48] At the third annual NEASS meeting, held in January 1835 at Boston's Julien Hall, "hundreds of persons who came to the door, were forced to retire without being able to enter" when the choir performed at the evening session on 21 January. According to the association minutes, the event came to an official close when the "Colored Juvenile Choir, under the direction of Miss Paul," sang "several hymns suited to the occasion" in the auditorium that was "crowded to suffocation."[49]

Susan Paul's race and gender afforded her little protection in the American public sphere. Still, she managed to deliver, on many occasions, a public political message, a series of memorable, powerful, and evocative indictments of slavery, of colonization, of the compromised sugar trade, and of everyday prejudice, in large part because she never said a word. Her activism depended on babes, and her words came out of their mouths. The creation and deployment of an African American juvenile choir was a brilliant tactical move for a woman determined to advance her family's long-standing commitment to racial self-determination, passion for equal rights, and appreciation of God-given talents and poise.

Even in this seemingly successful collaboration with Garrison, Paul the abolitionist had to remain vigilant. In March 1834, Paul and Garrison engaged in a public debate that illuminated the fundamentals and pitfalls of emancipatory feminism. Their public tussle began as a result of unfortunate but typical prejudice against African Americans. The Juvenile Choir was engaged to sing at an NEASS-sponsored antislavery event at the Second Baptist Church in Salem. Indeed, their presence promised to increase attendance; Garrison would later note in the *Liberator* that "additional interest was imparted to [the] proceedings by the presence and performances of a number of colored children, under the direction of Miss Susan Paul, from Boston who were invited to attend, and sing a number of hymns selected for the occasion."[50] The real story should have focused on the fact that the students performed for an "overflowing house" and that there was a "vast concourse of spectators" who "expressed their gratification" through "repeated bursts of applause."[51] However, Garrison, in his report on the event, directed readers to the events preceding the choir's significant contribution to the abolitionist rally. The 29 March 1834 issue of the *Liberator* contained the following passage in the account of the Salem meeting:

Three coaches were engaged to carry Miss Paul and her juvenile choir to Salem; these were driven up to her door at the hour specified in the bargain, but as soon as the drivers discovered that the children were somewhat darker in complexion than themselves, they got into a rage, and profanely declared that 'they would be d——d if they were to carry a load of *niggers* in the best coaches of Boston—they would sooner have their throats cut from ear to ear'!!! So these highly polished, intelligent *gentlemen* indignantly mounted their seats, cracked their whips, and drove back to their appropriate home—the stable—having violated their contract and exhibited a meanness of conduct which places them far beneath the lowest slave in the country.[52]

Garrison insisted that such behavior revealed the "vulgar and criminal prejudices, which reign in New England against a colored complexion." Yet, his article, with its all-encompassing focus on the racist encounter and its neglect of the songs performed and the speeches delivered, left readers with the image of African American children not as a pioneering abolitionist force but as needy black children who required and would benefit enormously from increased antislavery activity—political action that was essentially coded as a call for increased white action. Paul interpreted Garrison's reorientation of the event as a serious challenge to her effort to help her students cultivate their own highly functional, resilient, and self-determined racial subjectivity. His report also threatened to undercut her efforts to maintain the unprecedented political agency that these children could claim as they mastered and communicated politically insightful assessments and indictments of antebellum American and international politics.

Paul used her pen and the *Liberator* to confirm her staunch grip on the standard of African American activism. Her "neatly written note" appeared quite promptly in the very next issue of the newspaper, and she systematically revealed the dangers and limitations of Garrison's perspective. Where he claimed that the children's treatment would have prompted their "Salem friends" to feel "indignation," she reminded him that such incidental outrage was a dubious privilege. African Americans could not luxuriate in such occasional responses: "We were not surprised at our treatment from these persons," she wrote. "This is but a faint picture of that spirit which persecutes us on account of our color—that cruel prejudice which deprives us of every privilege whereby we might elevate ourselves—and then absurdly condemns us because we are not more refined and intelligent."[53] The rhetorical and political might of Paul's observations was considerable. She swiftly deromanticized Garrison's graphic and dramatic description of the coachmen's response and defined it instead as a "faint" picture of the regular injustices she and other people of color had to endure. She also asserted herself boldly as an NEASS member; her comments about the "cruel prejudice" that both deprives African Americans and then condemns them for their lack reaffirmed the very need for and value of an organization such as the NEASS, one that authored noble and necessary constitutions that enabled members to pledge their commitment to achieving real social justice and racial progress. If Garrison used the encounter with the coachmen to essentially compliment and entice Salemites to ally with him, Paul used the same scene to offer a Stewart-esque rallying cry to white abolitionists. "This is no time to despair," she counseled. "The rapid progress of the cause which you so successfully advocate will, ere long, annihilate the present corrupt state of things, and substitute liberty and its concomitant blessings."[54] Finally, Paul underscored the extensive and enabling African American network that functioned independent of and in tandem with white abolitionists. John Remond, an NEASS colleague of Paul's and the legendary Salem caterer whose children Charles and Sarah became leading African American antislavery lecturers, feted her and the choir. "A sumptuous entertainment was provided for the children at the residence of Mr. Remond, and each member of the family did all in their power to contribute to our happiness," Paul reported with an air of considerable pride. In the Remond home, the children received, in addition to bodily nourishment, political, emotional, and racial sustenance, a benefit that enabled Paul to reclaim for her choir and the race they represented a more powerful, steady, and enabling African American activist context.

In late 1833, as Paul was crafting the intriguing public abolitionist campaign she would initiate as an NEASS member, she and Garrison collaborated on yet another meaningful emancipatory and feminist mission. This time the focus was on an organization in which Boston and the antislavery North could take pride, the Boston Female Anti-Slavery Society (BFASS). Founded in October 1833 by twelve white women of Quaker, Unitarian, Baptist, and Congregational affiliations, BFASS was the city's premier ladies' abolitionist group. Yet, in a city that was home to such honorable women as Susan Paul, her mother, Catherine Paul, and such intrepid activists as Nancy Prince, BFASS was formed and began its institutional life as a whites-only society. Historians have tended to regard the group as one of the forward thinking, racially integrated antebellum societies. However, it integrated itself only after Garrison berated members for being "influence[d] by the common, (and no less criminal than common) prejudice of community" and apparently "resolved to perpetuate the caste of color."[55] Members were aghast at the notion that its exclusion of African American women might sully its reputation and detract from its stated mission to "wash away the guilt of Slavery from their *consciences,* and if possible, from the *world.*"[56]

Garrison's interventions often were informed and reinforced by carefully attended professional relationships with women at home and abroad. His connections to scholarly and politically astute women in international circles also make visible and contextualize further the import of his multifaceted emancipatory projects. The intervention Garrison deployed in his BFASS anti-segregation protest, for example, was one that Harriet Martineau would certainly have approved of (she was the acclaimed and intrepid British writer who in October 1835 was traveling by carriage through Boston to Providence, Rhode Island, when Garrison almost was lynched publicly). Martineau, who in 1841 published a highly regarded antislavery novel about Toussaint L'Ouverture entitled *The Hour and the Man: A Historical Romance,* was a keen observer of American abolitionist matters, and Garrison held her in high regard. He lauded her in an eponymous sonnet, published in his collection *Sonnets and Other Poems* (1843) as one whose "heart is large, whose spirit is sublime" and who was a "friend of liberty, of wrong the foe."[57] In a letter of October 1835 to his sister Mary Benson, Garrison referred to the enterprising British writer as "the distinguished authoress from England" and declared that she had "shown true moral courage in attending the meeting of the Boston Female Anti-Slavery Society, and avowing her approval of its principles."[58] After reading in the early 1840s of the split in American abolitionist organizations, Martineau reasoned that "it is our duty to expose their guilt when, by their act of compromise, they oppress and betray those brethren whose nobleness is a rebuke, to themselves. This painful duty may every friend of the negro in this country now find himself called upon to discharge, if he gives due attention to the state of anti-slavery affairs in America. If he does *not* give this attention, it would be better for him that he never named the negro and his cause; for it is surely better to stand aloof from a philanthropic enterprise than to mix up injustice with it."[59]

BFASS was an organization through which the founders "hope[d] to increase, and judiciously exert [their] strength and influence and contribute [their] proportion of moral power, toward wielding that weapon that is to exterminate slavery from [their] land."[60] In their early correspondence with other female antislavery societies, BFASS members admitted that an "astonishing apathy" about race matters had "prevailed" among them. After realizing that such complacency "cannot be desired," they committed themselves to "sleep no more" now that the "long, dark night is rapidly receding, the light of truth has unsealed our eyes, and fallen upon our hearts, [and] awakened our slumbering energies."[61] When Susan Paul was appearing with her Juvenile Choir at the NEASS meetings and crafting her unique public campaign against slavery in late 1833 and early 1834, however, BFASS members did not seize the opportunity to direct their newly awakened energies to offer her support.

The members of BFASS, who prided themselves on the suitable nature of women's involvement in auxiliary groups, may have thought Paul's NEASS membership suggested an unbecoming boldness and off-putting political elit- ism. Nonetheless, Paul's affiliation with and activity within that group clearly confirmed the extent to which she was committed to the cause of abolition and to African American uplift. That Paul both exposed the children of her com- munity to the adult abolitionist forums and then enlisted the children's aid in her fight against slavery also may have frustrated, and even offended, the white BFASS constituency. Paul's work with the children anticipated BFASS's effort to "influence some of the little hearts of New England" and "to preach to the next generation . . . the doctrine that 'all men are created free.' "[62] Paul's emergence as a public figure, however modified, mediated, and decorous, may have challenged those BFASS members who shied away from publicity and believed that women could work for the cause without appearing in public.

The most compelling explanation for BFASS's silence in the face of Paul's undisputed successes with the Juvenile Choir lies with the group's "unwilling- ness to admit colored females as members." Some BFASS members "[did] not hesitate to avow a strong aversion to those whose skins are 'not colored like their own.' "[63] In April 1834, the society invited Garrison to deliver an address at one of their meetings; he quickly declined and suggested to them that the membership use the time allocated for his lecture for another purpose. "It is my desire," he wrote to the society on 9 April 1834, "that you should freely discuss, and firmly settle, the principles upon which you are determined to act." He continued, admitting that he found it "strange . . . and glaringly paradoxical, that any person should join a society for the abolition of slavery, and yet to be themselves the slaves of a vulgar and insane prejudice, from which have sprung innumerable and grievous calamities to those who groan under the bondage of public opinion, or of Southern injustice." The society responded promptly, writing just two days later on 11 April 1834 to insist that Garrison's belief that the majority of members opposed an integrated society was "incorrect." Mary Grew, the corresponding secretary, asserted that "this was the feeling of but a few of us" and insisted that the group did "not merit an accusation as severe as this." She continued, stating, "I am happy to inform you that our decision was, on the side of justice" and "that we resolved to receive our colored friends into our Society, and immediately gave one of them a seat in our Board."[64] The woman to whom they had "thrown open the doors of the Society" was Susan Paul.

In 1835, the same year Garrison found himself careening madly through Bos- ton's narrow streets in order to avoid the murderous lynch mob composed of

"Boston Gentlemen," Angelina Grimké found herself compelled by Garrison's actions to realize in action the spirited thoughts she had shared with him. As August 1835 came to close, Grimké prepared to pay heavily for her investment in Garrisonian principles and noble rhetoric. As Katharine Du Pre Lumpkin notes in her biography of the South Carolinian, Grimké penned a letter to Garrison that would quite literally sever her ties with the South, forge new connections to the North, and position her at the forefront of women's abolition and American antislavery work. Lumpkin characterizes this turning point in poignant and wholly economic terms:

> For though she might not comprehend the full price she would pay, she was not unaware of a good measure of the cost: the cost as a daughter of her slaveowning mother, whom she knew she would wound beyond her power to heal; the cost as a sincere and respected Friend, who would be ostracized, perhaps disowned, because she was refusing to abide by the Friends' discipline; the cost as a woman, for deep in her heart she knew that the glaring restrictions that were placed on her sex stood between her and the work she felt called to; the cost as a sister, for on this occasion Angelina knew she was deliberately excluding Sarah from this most crucial and far-reaching act and, by doing so, was severing those bonds that had held her back from finding her own course.[65]

Grimké, embracing the principles of nonviolence that Garrison and his colleagues professed, declared herself a sister of the cause. In the letter she sent to Garrison from Philadelphia, which she saw again in printed form when her Quaker colleague James Bettle first showed her the *Liberator,* a newspaper he "scorned,"[66] Grimké offered a most eloquent call to arms, echoing the declaration Garrison himself had made in the debut issue of the *Liberator.* She noted first that her "mind has been especially turned toward those, who are standing in the forefront of the battle" and that she was praying "for *their* preservation — not the preservation of their lives, but the preservation of their minds in humility and patience, faith, hope, and *charity.*" Then, she offered the following explosive conviction: "If persecution is the means which God has ordained for the accomplishment of this great end, EMANCIPATION: then, in dependence *upon Him* for strength to bear it, I feel as if I could say, LET IT COME — let us suffer, rather than that insurrection should arise: for it is my deep, solemn, deliberate conviction, that *this is a cause worth dying for.* I say so, from what I have seen, and heard, and known, in a land of slavery. . . . Yes! LET IT COME — let us suffer, rather than that insurrection should arise."[67] The invocation of a political apocalypse that suffused Grimké's proclamation did not compromise her womanly influence. Some two years after Garrison had thrust her into the public abolitionist forum, he was praising her and her sister Sarah as "our gifted friends," insisting that they were "exerting an almost angelic influence wherever they go." In addition, Garrison insisted that "their triumph over prejudice and error has been most signal."[68] Some of the most compelling moments in which Garrison financed acts of bold emancipatory feminism reveal the extraordinary resilience of women. These individuals were subjected to various subversive and explicit campaigns of terror, but they persisted in the face of these challenges and produced certain evidence of women's ambition and the potential advancement of all.

William Lloyd Garrison insisted that his male antislavery colleagues be called to feminist accountability when he confronted directly the issue of full access for women within the ranks of the male-dominated antislavery organizations as well. As the years passed, the nineteenth-century women's abolitionist sphere — one governed by cultural ideals promoted by the "cult of true womanhood" — was expanding dramatically and in ways that improved the political power and abolitionist work of men. Women throughout New England and the North proved themselves to be tireless fund-raisers, creative in their plans for outreach, persistent in their sales of newspaper and abolitionist gift book subscriptions, and downright unstoppable in their efforts to secure signatures for petitions. Such work granted women, no matter how demure or subjugated they might be at home, a visible and powerful place in the political world. The work of women like Prudence Crandall, the other female lifetime NEASS member with Susan Paul, the editor Lydia Maria Child, the organizer Maria Weston Chapman, and others prompted a reevaluation of "true womanhood," which depended on the ideals of piety, purity, domesticity, and submissiveness. Garrison was well positioned to see the advancement of women, their steady encroachment, as some would define it, on the American political sphere. He respected the strength of character and unapologetic focus of women like Sojourner Truth, Abby Kelley, and Martha Wright. (Despite being six months pregnant, Wright journeyed by train from Auburn to Seneca Falls, New York, in the hot summer of 1848 to sign the Declaration of Sentiments that called for the full enfranchisement of women.)

In April 1840, Garrison, who was about to depart for London for a historic antislavery meeting, encouraged a friend who was setting off before him to be steady in his political resolve. "My dear [George] Bradburn," he wrote to his colleague, "it is not probable that I shall arrive in season to be at the opening of the Convention; but, I beseech you, *fail not to have women recognized as equal beings in it.* Interchange thoughts with dear [George] Thompson about it. I know he will go for humanity, irrespective of sex." Unfortunately, the British conference committee was going against sex, regardless of humanity, and had planned to provide a modest set of seats in a "side chamber" from which women like Lucretia Mott and Ann Phillips, the wife of Wendell Phillips, could listen to the proceedings. How can we argue for universal reforms, asked Garrison's energetic prowomen colleagues, when such seating arrangements constitute the "disenfranchising of one-half of creation."[69]

Garrison was in fine form when he arrived in England for the meeting. In his characteristically constructive-mischievous way, he decided that the balcony seats set aside for the ladies could be transformed from a marginalized perch into a central place of power. In that segregated place, Garrison sat with Charles Lenox Remond, the abolitionist lecturer from Salem, Massachusetts, the Phillipses of Boston, and even the widowed Lady Byron. He refused overtures from the conference committee to "come down" and prompted one attendee to conclude that the Americans — men and women sitting in close proximity — were a "glorious crew." "Garrison is one of God's nobility," decided Maria Waring, a relative of a prominent Irish leader, who was convinced she never had seen "such an angelic, holy-looking face" and that the "Garrisonians are strong and fine and firm . . . a new race of beings [who] regard women not as dolls but as human beings."[70]

Martineau reveled in Garrison's purposeful theatrics. He was, she wrote in a letter to her dear friend Chapman, Garrison's Boston ally and BFASS leader, "quite right, I think, to sit in the gallery at Convention." She assured her American friend that she was "persuaded" his actions had "done much for the woman question." The legendary standoff at the 1840 convention also gave visionary and ambitious women activists invaluable optimism. The events in London buoyed up Martineau, and she insisted that Chapman would "live to see a great enlargement of our scope" even though "the view of some women and the fears of others" made it difficult and "hard work for us to assert our liberty. I will however, till I die, and so will you; and so make it eager for some few to follow us than it was for poor Mary Wollstonecraft to begin."[71]

On American shores that same spring, Garrison was immersed in similar struggles to accord women a place of respect and unmediated access to antislavery work. The American Anti-Slavery Society (AASS) was embattled. At issue was whether or not its women members should be allowed to speak at meetings and vote on society matters. As Sherry Penney and James Livingston have noted in their biography of Martha Wright, it was the nomination of Abbey Kelley, the future wife of the abolitionist Stephen S. Foster, to the AASS business committee that had sparked foment in that organization. In May 1840, as the controversy raged, one member, Elizur Wright, put it in husbandry terms that recalled Samuel Johnson's oft-quoted remark equating women's speaking with dogs tottering on their hind legs. The antislavery man

Elizur Wright declared he was "opposed to hens crowing" and preferred that "the tom turkeys . . . do the gobbling."[72]

Garrison and his cohort of prowomen members prevailed against what the biographer Mayer describes quite delightfully as the "starchy 'protest'" of individuals such as Lewis Tappan, who believed that the increasingly public and equal roles of women were "well suited to bring *unnecessary* reproach and embarrassment to the cause of the enslaved, inasmuch as it is at variance with general usage and sentiments of this and all other nations."[73] Tappan's reservations confirmed attitudes that we continue to recognize today, namely, that in some American quarters there still are limits and lingering gender-restrictive notions of who best is fitted to lead — whether it be universities, corporations, or nations. Indeed, in the aftermath of Kelley Foster's election to the committee, two members asked to be released from their places on that board, and members who opposed the entire venture protested by leaving the meeting and sometime later forming the American and Foreign Anti-Slavery Society, an entirely separate organization.

In the post–Civil War years, Garrison's liberatory ethos was hard-pressed by the expectations of dedicated abolitionists and women suffragists like Elizabeth Cady Stanton and Susan B. Anthony. It was the prospect of legislative action that resurrected the antebellum logic of racialized emancipatory feminism that Garrison had applied with great success. As debates intensified about the Fourteenth and Fifteenth Amendments, it became clear that advocacy of civic freedom and political justice for African American men would polarize members of the old abolitionist alliances. Stanton was deeply frustrated by Garrison and other stalwarts of the abolitionist movement who had advocated for women's full participation in their antebellum organizations but who now reasoned, as Wendell Phillips did in at least one exchange with Stanton, that in the current debate about African Americans and suffrage, they could not "have a coach with uneven wheels." This was not the time, explained Phillips, to have a campaign that lobbied for the vote for African American men and also called for the full acknowledgment of all American women. Phillips believed that a "mixture" of the two issues "would lose for the Negro far more than we should gain for the woman." As Stanton's biographer Elisabeth Griffith notes, "In order to abolish slavery, Phillips and the abolitionists insisted on recognizing Negro citizenship, 'where citizenship supposes the ballot for all men.'" An angry Stanton shot back, "May I ask in reply to your fallacious letter just one question based on the apparent opposition in which you place the Negro and woman. My question is: Do you believe the African race is composed entirely of males?"[74] It was a chilling moment for Stanton, Anthony, and their colleagues, and one that Anthony dissected in terms that both confirmed the tenets of Garrisonian emancipatory feminism and illustrated the realities that plagued those who practiced it. It exemplified the inescapable bind and unsettling truth to which David Brion Davis refers in his essay "Slavery and the American Mind": "All idealism is compromised by tactical expediency, and all opportunism, no matter how ruthless, is compromised and rationalized by ideals."[75] "The real fact," stated Anthony, "is that we have so long held woman's claims in abeyance to the Negro's that the naming of them now is reckoned an impertinence."[76] Stanton was in some ways bedeviled. As a stalwart abolitionist she had protested Garrison's move in May 1864 to disband the AASS once the Thirteenth Amendment passed; she believed, as Griffith points out, that "the work was incomplete until the slaves had been made citizens and enfranchised."[77] Ultimately, the women's movement split, much as the abolitionist ranks divided over the woman question in 1840. In May 1869 Stanton and Anthony created the National Woman Suffrage Association, the group that in 1872 nominated the nation's first woman presidential candidate. Garrison stalwarts like Kelley Foster, Lucy Stone, and Louisa May Alcott supported the New England Woman Suffrage Association, which advocated female suffrage and supported passage of the Fifteenth Amendment.[78]

Garrison published his farewell address on 29 December 1865, in the final issue of the *Liberator.* By that time, promising organizations such as the NEASS and BFASS had fallen prey to major differences of opinion among members, evolved into different organizations, and otherwise signaled by their change or absolution the bittersweet progress that signals a society's growth, evolution, and retrenchment. The energetic abolitionist editor lived for fourteen years after the Civil War came to its bloody and hard-won close in the spring of 1865. In May 1879, hundreds turned out for his funeral, an occasion that saw Theodore Weld deliver stirring remarks about his fallen friend. Weld savored with those gathered in Boston's Eliot Square sanctuary of the First Religious Society of Roxbury the awe-inspiring ways in which Garrison constituted a true "army of one." The life of this abolitionist printer, tireless leader, and devoted father, Weld mused, illustrated "how, when one soul is . . . stirred in its innermost and to its uttermost, it is irresistible." Garrison's power lay in his ability to encourage "souls, here and there, and thick and fast, too, not merely one, and another, and another, of the great mass, but multitudes of souls . . . to receive the truth and welcome it, to incorporate it into their thought and feeling, to live and die for it."[79] That animation, which Garrison so effectively achieved, contributed significantly to the steady advances American women made for themselves and on behalf of others as the nineteenth century continued to unfold.

Weld urged those assembled at Garrison's funeral to "think for a moment of Garrison" and the ways in which, "through his paper and by his speech, traversing the country, [he] utter[ed] words which fell with such force as to break the spell that was upon souls, rouse the latent and dormant and bring them to life, gird them with power, and put weapons into their hands, arming them from head to foot, to go forth and fight in the moral warfare!"[80] This description of a holy political baptism lies at the heart of the emancipatory feminist work that Garrison advocated in his outreach to Maria Stewart, Angelina Grimké, organizers of the 1848 Seneca Falls convention, and the nameless ordinary women who formed moral societies and female antislavery groups in the name of "freedom and justice" even as they grappled with the implications of what that might mean "for all." In 1879, Weld lingered in his contemplation of Garrison's powers to awaken others to action; this notion of vital animation also provides an appropriate way to consider the emancipatory feminist exercises that women like Susan Paul urged Garrison to complete for his own sake and for that of the cause.

Throughout the antebellum era, Garrison addressed the challenges rising from his need to insist on the racial agenda of abolition and thus to preserve, at all costs, the original intent of his emancipatory political work. In striving to achieve this, Garrison challenged women on both sides of the color line to recognize that their own liberation depended not on the revision of the marriage relationship, but on their ability to become unerring advocates of African emancipation and racial equality. He proposed an imposing and transformative agenda but did so because he regarded it as one essential to the success of immediate abolition. Gradualism and diluted activism transported all into a realm of delay, into a province of obfuscation and distraction that so easily accommodated the ranking of pressing social and political issues such as women's suffrage, educational segregation, and marriage rights.

In 1855, Charlotte Forten, one of his youngest admirers, mused in her diary about Garrison's commitment to the ladies and to justice when she found herself unable to reach Boston for the twentieth-anniversary commemorations of the antislavery riot there that culminated in Garrison's sequestering in the Leverett Street Jail. Forten was steadied by the fact that "to-day on the very spot where that little band of noble-hearted women so heroically maintained the right, the dauntless Pioneer of our glorious cause stands with many true-hearted co-workers, surrounded by hundreds of eager, sympathizing listeners."[81] Forten's romantic tribute to Garrison and to BFASS, the group that included Susan Paul, the Weston sisters, and other women of color such as Julia Williams, was intense. It also reveals an ethereal but nevertheless tangible example of how Garrison became an integral part of the effort to achieve and to protect the advancement of women. That Forten, an impressionable young girl of eighteen, could write so stirringly of an event that happened before her birth and that clearly shaped her feminist sensibilities and political convictions confirms the far-reaching power of Garrison's actions. Indeed, his unerring and lengthy emphasis on humanity — not simply or only manhood — was what helped to keep alive the prospect of women's full participation and recognized leadership in the fight for civil rights and equity.

In 1831, Garrison declared that he was " ready, on all days, on all convenient occasions, in all suitable places, before any sect or party, at whatever peril to my person, character or interest, to plead the cause of my colored countrymen in particular, or of human rights in general. For this purpose, there is no day too holy, no place improper, no body of men too inconsiderable to address."[82] The deliberate manner in which he cultivated connections with women and sought out the historically marginalized and silenced testifies to his sincere effort to "plead the cause" of "human rights." His commitment to the advancement of women was not expressed in hollow rhetorical flourishes. His emancipatory feminism was enhanced by his characteristic eloquence and confirmed by his willingness to become what Forten so eloquently called him: "a dauntless crusader" of the "glorious cause."

Notes

1. William Lloyd Garrison, *Liberator*, 1 January 1831.

2. William Lloyd Garrison to Elizabeth Pease, 6 November 1837, in Louis Ruchames, ed., *The Letters of William Lloyd Garrison*, vol. 2: *A House Dividing Against Itself, 1836–1840* (Cambridge: Harvard University Press, 1971), 326.

3. L. H. Butterfield et al., eds., *Adams Family Correspondence*, 4 volumes (Cambridge, Mass.: 1963), 1:370, Mar. 31, 1776.

4. See Elaine Forman Crane, "Political Dialogue and the Spring of Abigail's Discontent," *William and Mary Quarterly* 56.4 (October 1999): 745–74.

5. Mark Kann, *The Gendering of American Politics: Founding Mothers, Founding Fathers, and Political Patriarchy* (Westport, Conn.: Praeger, 1999), 3.

6. Susan Zaeske, *Signatures of Citizenship: Petitioning, Antislavery, and Women's Political Identity* (Chapel Hill: University of North Carolina Press, 2003), 1–2.

7. William Lloyd Garrison to Helen E. Garrison, 25 May 1836, in Ruchames, *The Letters of William Lloyd Garrison*, 2:109.

8. Elisabeth Griffith, *In Her Own Right: The Life of Elizabeth Cady Stanton* (New York: Oxford University Press, 1984), 41.

9. Henry Mayer, "William Lloyd Garrison: The Undisputed Master of the Cause of Negro Liberation," *Journal of Blacks in Higher Education* 23 (Spring 1999): 106.

10. Julie Roy Jeffrey, *The Great Silent Army of Abolitionism: Ordinary Women in the Antislavery Movement* (Chapel Hill: University of North Carolina Press, 1998), 53.

11. Ibid., 54.

12. Garrison, *Life of William Lloyd Garrison* (New York, 1885–89), 3:390.

13. "Sorrows of a Female Heart" by Charlotte, *Liberator*, 31 March 1832.

14. William Lloyd Garrison to Helen E. Garrison, 30 May 1836, in Ruchames, *The Letters of William Lloyd Garrison*, 2:115.

15. Henry Mayer, *All on Fire: William Lloyd Garrison and the Abolition of Slavery* (New York: St. Martin's Press, 1998), 265.

16. Stacey M. Robertson, *Parker Pillsbury: Radical Abolitionist, Male Feminist* (Ithaca: Cornell University Press, 2000), 28.

17. Bonnie Anderson, *Joyous Greetings: The First International Women's Movement, 1830–1860* (New York: Oxford University Press, 2000), 122.

18. Ellen Weinauer, "A Most Respectable Looking Gentleman': Passing, Possession, and Transgression in *Running A Thousand Miles for Freedom*," in Elaine Ginsberg, ed., *Passing and the Fictions of Identity* (Durham: Duke University Press, 1996), 39. For additional considerations of Rose's critique of patriarchal economics and power and women's subjugation, see Carol Kolmerten, *The American Life of Ernestine L. Rose* (Syracuse: Syracuse University Press, 1999); Ellen Carol DuBois, "Outgrowing the Compact of the Fathers: Equal Rights, Woman Suffrage, and the United States Constitution, 1820–1878," *Journal of American History* 74.3, 836–62; and Norma Basch, "Invisible Women: The Legal Fiction of Marital Unity in Nineteenth-Century America," *Feminist Studies* 5.2 (Summer 1979): 346–66.

19. Foner, "The Meaning of Freedom in the Age of Emancipation," *Journal of American History* 81, no. 2 (1994): 435–60.

20. Louise Michele Newman, *White Women's Rights: The Racial Origins of Feminism in the United States* (New York: Oxford University Press, 1999), 5.

21. Cited in Foner, "The Meaning of Freedom," 444.

22. Ibid., 450.

23. Amy Dru Stanley, *From Bondage to Contract: Wage Labor, Marriage, and the Market in the Age of Slave Emancipation* (Cambridge: Cambridge University Press, 1998), 176.

24. Jean Fagan Yellin, *Women and Sisters: The Anti-Slavery Feminists in American Culture* (New Haven: Yale University Press, 1989), 79.

25. Ibid., 79.

26. *Liberator*, 21 July 1832.

27. Yellin, *Women and Sisters*, 79.

28. Ibid., 79.

29. Jeffrey, *The Great Silent Army of Abolitionism*, 39.

30. Sarah P. Remond, "Speech by Sarah P. Remond Delivered at the Music Hall, Warrington, England, 24 January 1859," in C. Peter Ripley, ed., *The Black Abolitionist Papers*, vol. 1 (Chapel Hill: University of North Carolina Press, 1985), 438. For more information about Remond, see Sibyl Ventress Brownlee, "Out of the Abundance of the Heart: Sarah Ann Parker Remond's Quest for Freedom" (Diss., University of Massachusetts at Amherst, 1997).

31. Stanley, *From Bondage to Contract*, 179.

32. Ibid., 177.

33. Dorothy Courtnay Bass, " 'The Best Hope of the Sexes': The Woman Question in Garrisonian Abolitionism" (Ph.D. diss., Brown University, 1980), 46. Cited in Jeffrey, *The Great Silent Army of Abolitionism*, 39, 41.

34. Ellen DuBois, *Feminism and Suffrage: The Emergence of an Independent Women's Movement in America, 1848–1869* (Ithaca: Cornell University Press, 1985), 71. For more information about Lucy Stone, see Andrea Moore Kerr, *Speaking Out for Equality* (New Brunswick: Rutgers University Press, 1992), and Elinor Rice Hays, *Morning Star: A Biography of Lucy Stone, 1818–1893* (New York: Octagon Books, 1978), and Leslie Wheeler, ed., *Loving Warriors: Selected Letters of Lucy Stone and Henry B. Blackwell, 1853 to 1893* (New York: Dial Press, 1981).

35. Robert E. Riegel, "The Split of the Feminist Movement in 1869," *Mississippi Valley Historical Review* 49(3) (December 1962): 486.

36. DuBois, *Feminism and Suffrage*, 52.

37. Ibid., 53.

38. Newman, *White Women's Rights*, 5.

39. Elizabeth Cady Stanton, "Address to the National Woman Suffrage Convention," Washington, D.C., January 19, 1869, reprinted in Mari Jo Buhle and Paul Buhle, eds., *The Concise History of Woman Suffrage: Selections from the Classic Work of Stanton, Anthony, Gage and Harper* (Urbana: University of Illinois Press, 1978), 254. Cited in Newman, *White Women's Rights*, 5.

40. William Lloyd Garrison, "The Marriage Question," *Liberator*, 17 November 1832.

41. "The Colored Mother of New England," *Liberator*, 6 July 1833; essays by members of the Society of Colored Ladies in Providence, *Liberator*, 22 September 1832.

42. *Ninth Annual Report of the Board of Managers of the Massachusetts Anti-Slavery Society, Presented January 27, 1841. With an Appendix,* in *Annual Report: Massachusetts Anti-Slavery Society*, vol. 1 (Westport, Conn.: Negro Universities Press, 1970), 16. The NEASS reorganized itself and adopted the name Massachusetts Anti-Slavery Society in 1837.

43. Lois Brown, "Out of the Mouths of Babes: The Abolitionist Campaign of Susan Paul and the Colored Juvenile Choir of Boston," *New England Quarterly* (March 2002): 60.

44. Maria Stewart, "*Farewell Address*," 69.

45. *Proceedings of the New-England Anti-Slavery Society at Its First Annual Meeting,* in *Annual Report: Massachusetts Anti-Slavery Society*, vol. 1 (Westport, Conn.: Negro Universities Press, 1970), 13.

46. Susan Paul of Boston, Prince Farmer, an oyster seller of Salem, and John Remond, a caterer and barber in Salem and the father of the pioneering abolitionist lecturers Charles and Sarah Parker Remond, were the first African Americans listed in NEASS membership roles. Other early African American members included the Reverend Samuel Snowden of Boston, who served as a counsellor. In 1833, the Boston-based Massachusetts General Colored Association successfully applied to become an auxiliary affiliate of the NEASS. That organization, headed by Thomas Dalton as president, William Cooper Nell as vice president, and James Barbadoes as secretary, enabled the NEASS to establish formal relations with a segment of Boston's African American community.

47. *Liberator*, 15 March 1834, 42.

48. Ibid., 43.

49. *Third Annual Report of the Board of Managers of the New-England Anti-Slavery Society,* in *Annual Report: Massachusetts Anti-Slavery Society,* vol. 1 (Westport, Conn.: Negro Universities Press, 1970), 3.

50. *Liberator,* 29 March 1834, 51.

51. Ibid.

52. Ibid.

53. Susan Paul to William Lloyd Garrison, 1 April 1834, William Lloyd Garrison Papers, Boston Public Library, Boston.

54. Ibid.

55. William Lloyd Garrison to the Boston Female Anti-Slavery Society, 9 April 1834, Boston Female Anti-Slavery Society Papers, Massachusetts Historical Society, Boston.

56. Debra Gold Hansen, *Strained Sisterhood: Gender and Class in the Boston Female Anti-Slavery Society* (Amherst: University of Massachusetts Press, 1993), 46. Hansen cites *Liberator,* 3 January 1835. This sentiment is also included in the society's constitution, dated 1 April 1834.

57. William Lloyd Garrison, "Harriet Martineau," in *Sonnets and Other Poems* (Boston: Oliver Johnson, 1843). Cited in Susan Belasco, "Harriet Martineau's Black Hero and the American Antislavery Movement," *Nineteenth-Century Literature* 55.2 (September 2000): 177.

58. William Lloyd Garrison to Mary Benson, 27 November 1835, in Walter E. Merrill, ed., *The Letters of William Lloyd Garrison,* vol. 1: *I Will Be Heard! 1822–1835* (Cambridge: Harvard University Press, 1971), 564.

59. Harriet Martineau to Maria Weston Chapman, in *Harriet Martineau's Autobiography and Memorials of Harriet Martineau* by Harriet Martineau and Maria Weston Chapman (Boston, James R. Osgood, 1877), 353–54.

60. Boston Female Anti-Slavery Society to Reading Female Anti-Slavery Society, May 17, 1834, BFASS Papers, Massachusetts Historical Society.

61. Ibid.

62. BFASS to Concord, New Hampshire Female Anti-Slavery Society, July 22, 1835, BFASS Papers, MHS.

63. William Lloyd Garrison to BFASS, 9 April 1834, BFASS Papers, MHS.

64. Mary Grew to William Lloyd Garrison, 11 April 1835, BFASS Papers, MHS.

65. Katharine Du Pre Lumpkin, *The Emancipation of Angelina Grimké* (Chapel Hill: University of North Carolina Press, 1974), 83.

66. Ibid., 85.

67. Ibid., 83.

68. William Lloyd Garrison to Elizabeth Pease, 6 November 1837, in Ruchames, ed., *The Letters of William Lloyd Garrison, Volume II,* 326.

69. Mayer, *All on Fire,* 291.

70. Ibid.

71. Martineau to Chapman, in *Harriet Martineau's Autobiography and Memorials,* 350.

72. Mayer, *All on Fire,* 266. Contemporary scholarship on Kelley includes Dorothy Sterling, *Ahead of Her Time: Abby Kelley and the Politics of Anti-Slavery* (New York: W. W. Norton, 1991).

73. Ibid., 267.

74. Elisabeth Griffith, *In Her Own Right: The Life of Elizabeth Cady Stanton* (New York: Oxford University Press, 1984), 123.

75. David Brion Davis, "Slavery and the American Mind," in *Perspectives and Irony in American Slavery: Essays Edited by John W. Blassingame, David Brion Davis, Carl N. Degler, Stanley L. Engerman, Eugene D. Genovese, Harry P. Owens, William K. Scarborough, Kenneth M. Stampp* (Jackson: University Press of Mississippi, 1976), 52.

76. Mayer, *All on Fire,* 608.

77. Griffith, *In Her Own Right,* 122.

78. NEWSA metamorphosed into the American Women's Suffrage Association, and the new organization benefited from Garrison's support when he provided editorial input on *Woman's Journal,* its official publication.

79. Theodore Weld, "Remarks of Theodore Weld," in Louis Ruchames, ed., *The Abolitionists: A Collection of Their Writings* (New York: G. P. Putnam's Sons, 1963), 251.

80. Ibid., 252.

81. Charlotte Forten, diary entry for Sunday, 21 October 1855, in Brenda Stevenson, ed., *The Journals of Charlotte Forten Grimké* (New York: Oxford University Press, 1988), 141–42.

82. William Lloyd Garrison, "Words of Encouragement to the Oppressed" in Ruchames, *The Abolitionists,* 38.

4

Putting Politics Back In:
Rethinking the Problem of Political Abolitionism

BRUCE LAURIE

No observer of Massachusetts politics had ever seen anything quite like the legislative session of 1843. The General Court, as the house and senate were formally known, took action on civil rights that more than justified the Bay State's reputation as the most racially liberal state in the Union. Early in the session lawmakers repealed two laws, passed in 1705 and 1786, prohibiting marriage between Caucasians and peoples of color.[1] Legislators also passed a personal liberty law, popularly known as the Latimer Law, which denied federal officials tracking down fugitive slaves the use of Bay State jails and other public facilities.[2] Lawmakers, in addition, reintroduced a measure narrowly defeated the previous year prohibiting separate facilities on railroads by ending the recent invention of the Jim Crow "dirt car" for African American passengers. The revised bill went down in the house (having cleared the senate) but with the understanding that carriers would integrate their lines voluntarily instead of submitting to state mandate.[3]

The Liberty Party, the nation's first political party dedicated to emancipation, had a major role in the making of those civil rights initiatives. The party's founders included onetime Garrisonians convinced that moral suasion had reached its limits and that electoral politics was necessary. Invoking the Liberty Party in this context, or indeed any other, is likely to raise historians' eyebrows, for two reasons. We hardly know the Libertyites because they have long been in the shadow of Garrison and the Garrisonians, the activists who have proved far more attractive to scholars. Garrisonians, after all, founded the white abolitionist movement in the antebellum era and took a heroic stand for civil rights in a period when most northerners preferred racial segregation and black subordination; not a few northern states also tried to expel blacks. For their part, the Libertyites had no Garrison, no leader as dynamic or voluble as the Great Agitator. Small wonder they remain largely unknown.

What we do know about the Libertyites, moreover, is not especially flattering. Gilbert H. Barnes, one of the first authoritative historians of abolitionism and one of the few to stress the importance of political abolitionism, wrote off the Liberty Party as a "pathetic residue" worthy of passing notice only.[4] He preferred the political abolitionism of Whiggery. Later historians writing in this spirit alternately attributed the party's alleged irrelevance to political inexperience or naiveté rooted in the idealistic anti-institutionalism of evangelical Protestantism.[5] They were guilty of a debilitating moral absolutism originally described by Liberty men themselves as "Bible politics" or "political antipolitics," a term later adopted by modern critics of the party.[6] Aileen Kraditor, picking up on this characterization, asserted that the Libertyites were "conceived in frustration and self-delusion, acted out a farce, and died in betrayal."[7] Several scholars, following a more optimistic line of reasoning put forth at the turn of the 1950s by Dwight L. Dumond, find the Libertyites operating quite effectively at the state and local levels.[8] No historian more fully developed this approach than Richard H. Sewell, who persuasively demonstrated that the Liberty Party deftly blended antislavery morality into political activism. "Liberty men" in national politics, he tells us, "looked upon their party as much as a vehicle for abolitionist propaganda and as an instrument of political power."[9]

The most recent work cleaves between following Sewell and Barnes. Jonathan H. Earle and Frederick J. Blue examine political abolitionists and political abolitionism from different but engaging perspectives. Earle traces the origins of political antislavery to the egalitarianism of Jacksonian radicalism and charts the work of his insurgents in third-party politics largely at the national level. Blue profiles ten antislavery activists before the Civil War. Both draw attention to more obscure antislavery advocates as well as to better-known figures and seek to restore political antislavery to its rightful place in the narrative of antebellum reform. They also correct the conventional wisdom that such insurgents — Free Soilers especially — were racist. It would appear that politics is back in the reassessment of antislavery.[10]

Much of the work in the Barnes tradition centers outside of New England. An account of the Liberty Party in Ohio and the Old Northwest anchors the party in evangelical pulpits, predictably arguing it was a "religious party, just as revisionist critics said" — Puritans in the Babylon of politics.[11] Another work in this spirit, on upstate New York, describes a more complex organization factionalized into pragmatists and idealists that embraced land reform and progressive taxation as well as antislavery and civil rights. At the same time, the party's grounding in "ecclesiastical abolitionism" blunted its capacity for compromise and deal making in the political arena.[12] The work of Henry Mayer reaches the same conclusion from a different perspective, subordinating religion to ideology and personality. Echoing Barnes's derisive assessment of the party as a whole, Mayer cast Libertyites not as churchmen but "conservatives" blinkered by a litany of personal failings: James Birney retained the "oligarchic planter's hauteur"; Henry Stanton was suspect for his "transparent ambition and reputation for mendacity"; Amos Phelps was "hot tempered" and "preoccupied with petty grievances." As for Elizur Wright, Jr., his "administrative talents far exceeded his literary gifts." Mayer goes on to chastise historians of political abolitionism for diverting attention from the Garrisonians after 1840, a puzzling claim given the vast body of literature centered on Garrisonianism during the 1840s.[13]

In this chapter I confirm two trends in the revisionist scholarship on the Liberty Party and, by extension, on abolitionism more broadly. The first is that the party was not a sideshow but a main event, however briefly, in Bay State politics. The second is that while the party tried to work with the Garrisonians, it was rebuffed and chastised on the grounds that political involvement amounted to tacit acceptance of slavery because the Constitution was a proslavery document.[14] Garrison's slogan "No Union with Slaveholders" and his program of encouraging secession erected an impregnable wall between his "old org" and the "new org." That wall, however, did not separate Garrison from political activism. A close reading of his *Liberator* and, more to the point, his annual reports for the Massachusetts Anti-Slavery Society (MASS) shows that he followed state and national politics ever more closely as the 1840s wore on. The annual reports of the MASS grew lengthier with such additional subsections as "The Democratic Party," "The Whig Party," "The Third Party," and so on.[15] Garrison continued to encourage such policies as petitioning (the movement's most effective tactic), questioning office seekers, and organizing mass protests against discrimination and Jim Crow. Make no mistake, Garrison promoted the struggle for civil rights despite recent effort to downplay his racial liberalism.[16] The Great Agitator was undeniably paternalistic but also the nation's most credentialed friend of civil rights.[17] His blind spot — discerning the means to achieve his goals — was tactical. Garrisonianism never rejected the use of mass action to influence politicians. What it did reject through the 1840s, apart from voting, was working with third parties, and with the Liberty Party especially. When Garrison spoke of influencing politicians, he meant Whig politicians. He never forgave the Libertyites for bolting the movement in 1839–40. His obsession with that "betrayal" nearly equaled his obsession with the sins of the colonizationists a decade before. As a result, he often sounded petty and vindictive. He missed a chance to broaden the base of abolitionism by working with men and women who differed with him on tactical matters but not on the objectives of civil rights and emancipation. He underestimated electoral politics and the Libertyites as well, turning his back on a party that proved to be a very effective pressure group. Liberty operatives swung political regulars to support policies some individuals endorsed but the parties as a whole would not have supported on their own. Garrison's sectarianism forced the Libertyites to go it alone, a path they blazed with some skill and acumen and one that opened the way to the Free Soilers and the antislavery parties of the 1850s.

Two additional points in a historiographical spirit inform this essay. The first is that Liberty activists were not egalitarians who believed that African Americans were the social, moral, and intellectual equals of whites. I have argued elsewhere in more length and will repeat here that they were integrationists in a qualified way and paternalists above all else. They were patronizing and condescending toward blacks, just as Garrison was. Like him, they promoted integrating public accommodations partly because they saw segregation as an embarrassing remnant of slavery in their own backyard, not simply the etiquette of a distant region they had come to regard with greater and greater disdain.[18] Libertyites also believed that the state constitution at least guaranteed equal rights, if not outright equality; they were convinced that the federal Constitution could be enlisted in the struggle for emancipation and equality — and much earlier than most historians want us to believe. In 1841, four years before the more famous polemics of William Goodell and Lysander Spooner, the Boston chemist George W. F. Mellen took a similar position in *An argument on the unconstitutionality of slavery*, which he sent to Garrison for assessment; Garrison pronounced it "interesting" but not interesting enough to command his endorsement.[19] They also endorsed integration because they feared racial separatism was the crucible of black separatism and because they believed integrating blacks into white institutions and the schools especially would cleanse the objectionable features of their culture and make them more like whites in language, appearance, and aspiration. If that does not make them full-blown egalitarians, it also does not justify lumping them together with racists working for greater segregation or (neo)colonization.

The other point has to do with our persistent ignorance of abolitionists, both black and white, outside of the Garrisonian circle. Much of the literature

—too much I would say—follows Garrison and as a result leads away from the activists described above because they repudiated Garrisonian nonresistance for electoral politics. Not a single modern biography of Garrison pays much attention to the laws mentioned at the beginning of this chapter. The long shadow of Garrison has not only kept lesser figures in the dark; it has also made it difficult for scholars to take the Liberty Party seriously. Very few recognize the racial liberalism they passed on to the Free Soil Party, their successor in the politics of civil rights and antislavery. Important though Garrison was, the movement was much bigger than he through the 1840s. In fact, Garrisonianism and Libertyism were headed in opposite directions, the latter eclipsing the former and arguably having a greater impact in politics.

The Libertyites' image as bumbling amateurs traces in large part to their initial campaign in 1840. They entered the Bay State hustings with little or no organization, not much of a press, and an embarrassingly fluid ticket. Their nominee for governor stood down because he said he didn't believe in third-party politics; then his replacement (Roger Leavitt) suddenly died, leaving the top of the ticket blank. It was filled in at the last minute by a Whig who was persuaded to run by a loose group of aspiring leaders in accord on little else.[20] Within a few years, however, the new party began to resemble a serious political organization with a network of committees reaching down to the precincts, along with a major organ (Joshua Leavitt's *Emancipator*) and newspapers in just about every county in the state. It also boasted an impressive cadre of leaders, including Samuel Edmund Sewall, a lawyer by profession and the party's favorite gubernatorial nominee, as well as Henry Ingersoll Bowditch, a public health physician and party leader in Boston. Though Sewall and Bowditch enjoyed Brahmin pedigrees, such secondary leaders as Elizur Wright and Chauncey Langdon Knapp had more common origins in hardscrabble New England. Wright, the former corresponding secretary of the American Anti-Slavery Society and apostate Garrisonian, became a party journalist working with labor advocates like Knapp to bring the organization around to labor reform. It supported the fledgling movement for ten-hour workdays in industrial towns, including Lowell, where Knapp was the party's nominee for the General Court in the middle of the decade.[21] Knapp's foray into electoral politics indicates the importance of probing beyond the Liberty Party's formal policy of one-idea antislavery to what its operatives actually did in the districts. They ran best in the industrializing villages of the countryside, cobbling up a base of small shopkeepers and working people—plebeians, in a word.[22]

Libertyism, it is important to add, was not confined to white men. It also had the support of women who overlooked the antifeminism of Wright and of the many conservative clergymen in Congregational churches no more eager than Wright to work with women who stepped out of their sphere.[23] The Boston Female Anti-Slavery Society in May 1840 voted overwhelmingly (142–10) to leave their Garrison affiliate and re-form as the new org Massachusetts Female Emancipation Society because of their dismay over the old organization's "*no-government* friends."[24] Women abolitionists in the country, where the Liberty Party was much stronger than in the Hub City, were even more likely to pitch in. Mary White in the Worcester County village of Boylston certainly was. She told of enthusiasm for the "Abolitionist Ticket" in her town, explaining that her Congregationalist preacher used his Sabbath pulpit to call for "repentance on the importance of choosing good rulers and putting away slavery." His evening meeting was "mainly of politics," she said, assuming that the morning was not, and adding in her own words, "May the Lord direct the electing of this nation that slavery and oppression may cease."[25]

African Americans also came on board. Not long after the party formed, it was endorsed by *The Colored American*, Samuel Cornish's sheet in New York, and by at least one major African American church upstate in Albany.[26] Of course, many African Americans and especially those in the Bay State were personally loyal to Garrison and, at first, fiercely supportive of his antipathy to the new party. The more intrepid of them, like Frederick Douglass and Charles Lenox Remond, bore the banner of their hero even on hostile terrain. The meeting of the National Negro Convention in Buffalo in 1843, best remembered for the dramatic confrontation between Douglass and Henry Highland Garnet over militancy, passed a little-recognized resolution endorsing the Liberty Party.[27] The lone dissenters were Douglass and Remond, but they should not be mistaken for the voice of Bay State blacks.[28] The Boston civil rights leader Jehiel C. Beman was a Libertyite early in the decade, and it is likely that the black lawyer Robert Morris was sympathetic as well.[29] Such leaders pursued what the historian Charles H. Wesley long ago described as the pragmatism of endorsing moral suasion *and* political action, working for the Liberty Party or for friendly regulars depending on which tack was likely to be more fruitful.[30] The New Yorkers believed the party could help them achieve their main objective of eliminating property qualifications that prevented blacks from voting. Many more were drawn in by the middle of the decade, when the national organization made a point of welcoming blacks and condemning racist policies.[31]

The party enjoyed steady growth through the first half of the 1840s, reaching its apogee of sixty-two thousand votes in the presidential election of 1844. This small total had a huge impact on the national race, throwing the election to the expansionist Democrat James K. Polk and setting the stage for the

Mexican War. A similar scenario played out later in Massachusetts, where the party grew rapidly, peaking in 1846 at about ten thousand votes (just under 10 percent of the total). It wound up having great leverage because state elections, like the national contests, tightened as Whigs saw their commanding majority of the 1830s recede in the 1840s. Even more important, Massachusetts was one of the few states in the Union that retained the majority rule requirement in order to win elections. Candidates for state offices who did not garner a majority of the vote had to face runoffs until they did; deadlocked races were determined by the General Court. Statewide elections were so closely contested that on three occasions — 1842, 1843, and 1845 — the Libertyites threw the choice of governor to the legislature.[32] That was the electoral context in which the legislature of 1843 addressed the issue of civil rights.

The Liberty Party might have run well in 1842 on its own, without assistance from external events. The insurgency got an unexpected lift from the tumult over George Latimer, the Virginia slave who in fall 1842 bolted for freedom with his wife by hiding in a ship bound for Boston. Latimer tried to blend in in the Hub City's black quarter, known as The Hill, but was spotted in October by his former master's agent, who had him arrested on the trumped-up charge of larceny and then alerted his owner, James Gray. When Gray appeared in court for an article of removal in accordance with the Fugitive Slave Law of 1793, Judge Joseph Story ordered Latimer detained until his owner produced evidence of title. But instead of returning to court, Gray allowed local abolitionists to buy Latimer's freedom.[33]

Latimer was not an isolated episode. It came between two tumults over runaway slaves in 1839 and 1845 in the countryside, which were broadly seen as companion chapters in the treachery of the Slave Power.[34] John Greenleaf Whittier, the Quaker poet from Amesbury and a Liberty operative, captured the larger meaning of slavery in his essay "The Black Man" (1845). Whittier opened his piece with an anecdote about John Fountain, a free black jailed in Virginia on suspicion of helping slaves escape. Fountain was released from custody on condition that he leave the state but had to flee an angry mob, leaving his wife and children in bondage. He went on a speaking tour to raise funds to secure their freedom, taking a break from a talk in Lowell in order to thank Whittier for his help. "It is in this way," Whittier wrote of Fountain but clearly with Latimer in mind, "that the terrible reality of slavery is brought home to the people in this section of the country. Occasionally a fugitive from oppression seeks shelter among us and reveals the horrors . . . of bondage. . . . As a result, we no longer regard slavery in the abstract."[35]

Latimer's arrest intensified the feud between the old org and new org forces, as each side organized to reap the political whirlwind. They formed separate

Latimer Committees, which ran on parallel tracks but also collided head-on. The Garrisonian committee, organized shortly after Latimer's arrest and led by Remond, William Cooper Nell, and others, proved ineffective. Its fund-raising stumbled, and its effort to enlist legal support for Latimer turned into an embarrassment because the Libertyite stalwart Sewall stole their thunder. Sewall brokered Latimer's release and paid for his freedom with funds raised by his party's Latimer Committee, headed by Henry Bowditch, William F. Channing, and Frederick Cabot, with help from Reverend Nathaniel Colver.[36] The committee also scheduled public protests and doubled as the editorial board of the *Latimer Journal and North Star,* an ephemeral party organ.

The work of the Libertyite committee angered Garrisonians, who denounced Sewall's intervention for Latimer as "compensation" for slavery.[37] Their pique thwarted Bowditch's best efforts to call a truce in the name of the beleaguered Latimer. The accommodating patrician included Garrisonians on the podium at a late October meeting, only to hear the gathering dissolve into disorder when Wendell Phillips rose to "CURSE. . . the Constitution."[38] Tempers were no cooler several weeks later at another "joint meeting" in celebration of Latimer's newfound freedom. The Garrisonians rejected a motion to put Colver on the business committee, electing Maria Chapman Weston instead. Colver stormed out; Leavitt denounced the "proscriptive spirit" born of the "OLD GRUDGE"; Bowditch openly despaired, then listened in amazement to gratuitous assaults on his party by the Garrison loyalists Phillips and Stephen Foster.[39]

Garrisonians sharpened their pens as the November 1842 race drew near. Garrison, in an election-eve editorial on the gubernatorial race, poured scorn on all candidates, dismissing the Whig John Davis as a surrogate for Henry Clay and the Democrat Marcus Morton as a shill for "Martin Van Buren, or John C. Calhoun." That left Sewall, who Garrison conceded was a "meritorious man" but also a misguided one and the dupe of "those who are waging a war of extermination against the American Anti-Slavery Society," a fatuous charge more reflective of Garrison's obsessions than of realities on the ground. He added, "We recommend to voting abolitionists to scatter their votes in all such cases," aiming to hit the Libertyites where it mattered most. But only a puny 180 of the faithful followed suit, leaving Garrison not a little humbled and without much to say except that the electorate had been "led astray."[40]

The race of 1842 was a banner outing for the Liberty Party, just as Garrison seems to have feared. Their statewide candidates drew an average of some six thousand votes, nearly doubling the vote (5.4 percent) of the previous year. The tally complicated the gubernatorial race and left dozens of house seats, sixteen senate seats, and six Congressional seats hanging for want of a majority. Runoffs in December gave the Libertyites at least six seats in the house, which yielded the balance of power because the regulars were evenly divided and each needed Libertyite help in order to fill the remaining seats in the senate, name the speaker, and elect the governor. The shadowy horse-trading that followed showed that the Libertyites were no longer a fringe or a party of the "flank," as their Whig detractors called them. Liberty electees went after the sixteen senate seats but soon fell back, ceding them to the Democrats and helping put a Democrat in the governor's chair. They also wound up with the trump card for speaker. They held out through four ballots before supporting H. A. Collins, a Whig from the abolitionist wing of his party; in return the Libertyites extracted from both parties the promise of favorable action on civil rights bills; those bills cleared the General Court the following spring.[41]

This is not to dismiss the work of the old org pressure on the General Court. Indeed, Garrison first called attention to the ancient intermarriage ban over a decade before repeal. An early *Liberator* editorial railed against the proscription as unjust, racist, and particularly objectionable because it traced to the old colony's slave code.[42] Such a "disgraceful badge of servitude," as he called it, was unworthy of a Christian republic and an anathema to Yankees.[43] At the end of the decade his followers responded with a petition campaign that grew more robust as the 1830s turned into the 1840s. Some nine thousand men and women had signed petitions by 1843, about double the number of signatures in 1838 when the drive kicked off. The politicians had to take heed.

And they did. Despite a feverish reaction by racist journalists and cartoonists from both parties in the cities, lawmakers debated repeal each year after 1838. Whig and Democrat unimpressed with the justice of the matter reflected a range of positions. Some felt it was not the business of government to dictate who could marry whom; others believed it was a nonissue since there was no chance that a Caucasian would even consider the possibility of wedding a person of color.[44] All of that aside, the fact remains that Garrisonian agitation aroused the public and the politicians.

The same could be said of the movement to integrate public carriers. The advent of commuter rail lines in the 1830s brought the "dirt car," the overland equivalent of separate outdoor facilities for African Americans on water carriers. Garrison found such policies as objectionable as the interracial marriage ban. In the late 1830s he faithfully reported racist policies of private carriers; in the early 1840s he publicized indignities suffered by black passengers, including Douglass and David Ruggles.[45] His followers in Lynn gathered often in early fall 1841, once to condemn the eviction of John A. Collins and Douglass for openly defying separate seating on the Eastern Railway. Another rally called for a fresh petition imploring lawmakers to "defend the colored people who may see fit to take their seats in the long cars, in the enjoyment of their rights" by taking legislative action — a position endorsed by the MASS.[46]

Thus, Garrison yielded to no one when it came to airing the injuries and injustice of racial segregation. When he proclaimed, "I will be heard," he meant it. When he said, "No Union with Slaveholders," he not only meant condemning the Constitution; he also meant no union with third parties because their very involvement in electoral politics made them complicit with slavery, a kind of guilt by association. Such a position effectively severed his faction of the movement from an important avenue of the struggle for emancipation and civil rights. Though not out of the game altogether, Garrison wound up on the sidelines at a critical moment in the remaking of the antislavery movement and in the hewing of the alternative path of electoral politics in order to break down the barriers of social (if not economic) segregation.

It goes without saying that old and new org abolitionists reacted differently to the session of 1843. In his annual report to the MASS Garrison intoned that his organization would stick to its policy of pressuring the regulars because it was palpably successful. This "two party" policy, he said, worked because it "shows that we obtained every thing for which we have asked (with the exception of the railway bill) by votes of members of both parties, without the expense of time and money involved in the inception and conducting of a third." He conceded that a "short-sighted politician for the Third Party" could take some credit for "a portion of these successes." Then he abruptly and characteristically changed course, arguing that "while we would not deny that the existence of that party may have had an apparent effect . . . still, knowing as we do the origin, character and malign influences of that movement towards our enterprise, we cannot admit that its *interference* was of any genuine benefit" (emphasis added). He ended with the blunt assertion that "we should have gained more than we have achieved through the two other parties, had it not been for the interposition of the Third Party."[47]

Liberty men demurred, no one more prominently than Joshua Leavitt, who was the source of a good deal of Garrison's bitterness over the split because he had refused to give up control of the *Emancipator*. Leavitt told his readers that the action of the lawmakers on the Latimer Bill had been "prompt, firm, thorough, and unanimous." Taking a broader view of the session, he wrote that it was "an edifying and encouraging sight" to see the various bills pass "without debate — as a matter of course, precisely like the pay roll or an order notice in regard to the change in town lines. . . . The Latimer Committee got all they asked." The movement got even more, for the General Court had repealed the "anti-Christian" marriage ban and warned the railways to "behave better" or face "no mercy next year."[48]

Such measures unquestionably enjoyed momentum fueled by old org agitation. Indeed, as we have seen, two of them — the marriage ban and railway bill — had come before lawmakers the previous year and earlier still in the case of the ban. The fact is, however, they failed until the Liberty men weighed in. It was they who brokered the deal that put across the two major civil rights bills of the session and extracted the understanding with the railroads that produced the objective of the third.

Thereafter the Liberty Party sometimes gained voices disillusioned with their former parties. George Bradburn was an antislavery Whig from Nantucket at that time who had been a leading advocate for repealing the intermarriage ban and integrating railway cars.[49] In 1844, he left the Whigs, possibly over its tepid position on civil rights, its unpopularity in his new North-Shore district, or both. Whatever the case, Bradburn was a Libertyite, a political fact that bothered Garrison because abolitionist regulars like him justified Garrison's two-party strategy. The editor belittled Bradburn's departure in a letter to Henry Wright just before the 1844 election. "Poor man!" he exclaimed, "there is more of the Politician than of the Christian in his composition."[50] But Bradburn's departure clearly weighed on Garrison, for he mentioned it two months later in a letter to Elizabeth Pease, and again several months later in another note, to Richard Webb, adding "These are *trying* times certainly."[51]

If Bradburn's addition did not help the party much in the State House, it was partly because Libertyism stalled not long after he went over. Its vote fluctuated within a narrow range between 1844 and 1845 before reaching its plateau in 1846 and then sliding back. Party operatives carried on through the second half of the 1840s at the local level in the villages and industrial towns.[52] As the work of Bowditch in Boston indicates, they also built on the foundation laid elsewhere earlier in the decade, a surprising finding indeed in light of the party's weakness in the Commonwealth's leading city. The public health physician had helped coordinate the statewide petition in support of the Latimer Bill. At the start of the 1843 session Bowditch and his friends ceremoniously rolled into the State House a great coil of paper two feet wide and nearly a half mile in length pasted with 230 petitions demanding approval of the bill. So much for the Libertyites' political ineptitude.[53]

By 1845 Bowditch was a fearless ally of African Americans in Boston who were about to renew a drive to close the city's black-only schools and open mainstream classrooms to their children. This is no place to review that struggle in its entirety. It is enough to say that the agitation, which had died down in the late 1830s, picked up in 1840 when William Cooper Nell started a movement to dismiss the white head of Abiel Smith School accused of abusing the students. It drew inspiration from the concurrent civil rights campaigns over intermarriage and integration and from efforts to close Jim Crow schools in Salem and Lowell.[54] Nell's group got nowhere petitioning school authorities to sack the offensive headmaster and then close his hated school. A meeting of African American parents angered by the inaction called for a boycott of the "caste schools" and then linked up with local Libertyites. They had every reason to do so. In 1845, roughly coincident with the beginning of the boycott, Bowditch's party called on the legislature to prohibit taxation for support of separate schools and to admit black students to mainstream classrooms.[55] Bowditch, now a member of the Boston School Committee, proved to be a rare voice of enlightenment on the racist body. In 1846 the committee made short work of another petition on the grounds that segregation enjoyed no less of a sanction than the "All Powerful Creator." Bowditch replied in a minority report, coauthored by his fellow abolitionist Edmund Jackson, that claimed separate education based on race violated equal rights guaranteed to all Bay Staters under their constitution and constituted a dangerous example that could be used to exclude anyone for any reason. Separate schools not only reflected white chauvinism and inferior education; they also abetted racism by condemning black youths to illiteracy, ignorance, and poverty, which in turn made them easy targets "for the most inveterate hater of . . . [the black] race." The report recommended the bold step of phasing out the Smith School and allowing black children to disperse among schools of their choice, an early version of school choice voted down by the school authorities.[56]

This initial assault on the ramparts of school segregation in Boston and in the towns failed to achieve immediate results. But it did help solidify a biracial coalition in Boston and elsewhere that would strengthen in time, culminating in the 1855 law integrating public education in the Bay State.[57] The important point to bear in mind is that while Garrisonians were involved in this initiative from the beginning, the Libertyites joined in at midpassage and along the way drew more and more African Americans into political participation, including use of the ballot box. That coalition proved stronger still in the Free Soil Party, the political force that replaced the Libertyites and that continues to be misunderstood as single-mindedly racist. But that's a story for a different time.

Much of this chapter applies to Massachusetts, the place I know best. How typical was the Bay State? — a fair question but one we cannot answer with much confidence at this time simply because we do not know. We do not know because we have not done the spadework. Past work on New York and Ohio, the two other strongholds of Libertyism, is dated or generally suffers from the traditional tendency of looking at the party exclusively from an evangelical lens or assessing it by Garrisonian standards. Such a standard stacks the case against Libertyism by showing (erroneously, I would argue) that it was not as correct as the old org because it didn't come out for emancipation until 1844 and 1845.[58] Put another way, it was largely a matter of not measuring up to Garrisonianism.

All that aside, what we need is work on how antislavery parties functioned at the state and local levels; we need to look at what they did as well as what they said. We ought not expect to learn from such work that Ohioans had second thoughts and decided to integrate their schools or that New Yorkers regretted the opportunity at their constitutional convention in 1846 to broaden the black franchise. The political rules and valence of political actors in such places differed from those of Massachusetts; it would be foolish to expect the same or a similar result. We might find that the unmistakable tendency of deepening racism in the two decades before the Civil War did not go unchallenged. We might find resistance because we have seen enough of it in this essay, and in the revisionist work of Jonathan H. Earle and Frederick J. Blue, to believe that the struggle for racial equality at that time was more impressive than the conventional wisdom would have us believe.[59]

Notes

1. For instance, Massachusetts Anti-Slavery Society (MASS), *Twelfth Annual Report* (1844), 5–6; Louis Ruchames, "Race, Marriage, and Abolition in Massachusetts," *Journal of Negro History* 40 (1955): 250–73; and Sara Dubow, " 'Not a Virtuous Woman Among Them': Political Culture, Antislavery Politics, and the Marriage Ban in Antebellum Massachusetts" (seminar paper, University of Massachusetts, 1995).

2. Massachusetts House of Representatives, House Doc. No. 41, "Fugitives from Slavery" (1843), and Bruce Laurie, *Beyond Garrison: Antislavery and Social Reform* (New York: Cambridge University Press, 2005), 76–80.

3. Ruchames, "Jim Crow Railroads in Massachusetts," and MASS, *Twelfth Annual Report* (1844), 6–8.

4. Gilbert Hobbs Barnes, *The Antislavery Impulse, 1830–1844* (New York: D. Appleton-Century, 1933), 176. Also ibid., 177, 81.

5. Alan M. Kraut, ed., *Crusaders and Compromisers: Essays on the Relationship of the Antislavery Struggle to the Antebellum Party System* (Westport, Conn.: Greenwood Press, 1983). Also Aileen Kraditor, "The Liberty and Free Soil Parties," in Arthur Schlesinger, Jr., ed., *History of U.S. Political Parties*, 4 vols. (New York: Chelsea House, 1973), 1:741–881, and John R. McKivigan, ed., *Abolitionism in American Politics and Government* (New York: Garland Publishers, 1999).

6. Kraut, *Crusaders and Compromisers*, 13 ff.

7. Kraditor, "Liberty and Free Soil Parties," 1:741.

8. Dwight L. Dumond, *Antislavery: The Crusade for Freedom in America* (Ann Arbor: University of Michigan Press, 1961), 290–304.

9. Richard H. Sewell, *Ballots for Freedom: Antislavery Politics in the United States, 1837–1860* (New York: Oxford University Press, 1976), 88.

10. Jonathan H. Earle, *Jacksonian Antislavery Politics and the Politics of Free Soil, 1824–1854* (Chapel Hill: University of North Carolina Press, 2004), and Frederick J. Blue, *No Taint of Compromise: Crusaders in Antislavery Politics* (Baton Rouge: Louisiana State University Press, 2005).

11. Vernon L. Volpe, *Forlorn Hope of Freedom: The Liberty Party in the Old Northwest, 1838–1848* (Kent, Ohio: Kent State University Press, 1990), xi.

12. Douglas M. Strong, *Perfectionist Politics: Abolition and the Religious Tensions of American Democracy* (Syracuse: Syracuse University Press, 1999).

13. Henry Mayer, *All on Fire: William Lloyd Garrison and the Abolition of Slavery* (New York: St. Martin's Press, 1998), 268.

14. MASS, *Eleventh Annual Report* (1843), 4–10. Also Mayer, *All on Fire*, 300–29; John L. Thomas, *The Liberator: William Lloyd Garrison* (Boston: Little, Brown, 1963), 305–37; and Walter M. Merrill, *Against Wind and Tide: A Biography of Wm Lloyd Garrison* (Cambridge: Harvard University Press, 1963), 200–214.

15. See MASS, *Annual Reports* (1840–50), *passim*.

16. See, for instance, John Stauffer, *The Black Hearts of Men: Racial Abolitionists and the Transformation of Race* (Cambridge: Harvard University Press, 2001).

17. The most convincing recent portrait of him on that score is Paul Goodman, *Of One Blood: Abolitionism and the Origins of Racial Equality* (Berkeley: University of California Press, 1998), esp. 54–64.

18. Laurie, *Beyond Garrison*, esp. 87–105.

19. George W. F. Mellen, *An argument on the unconstitutionality of slavery, embracing an abstract of the proceedings of the national and state conventions on this subject* (Boston: Saxton and Pierce, 1841; rpnt., New York: AMS Press, 1973). Also, Garrison to Henry C. Wright, Dec. 16, 1843, in Walter M. Merrill and Louis Ruchames, *The Letters of William Lloyd Garrison*, 6 vols. (Cambridge: Harvard University Press, 1971–81), 3:237–38. Also ibid., 2:727.

20. Reinhard O. Johnson, "The Liberty Party in Massachusetts: Antislavery Third Party Politics in the Bay State, 1840–1848," *Civil War History* 28 (Sept. 1982): 237–65.

21. Laurie, *Beyond Garrison*, 136–39.

22. Johnson, "Liberty Party in Massachusetts." Also Mark Voss-Hubbard, "Slavery, Capitalism, and the Middling Sorts: The Rank and File of Political Abolitionism," *American Nineteenth-Century History* 4 (Summer 2003): 53–76, and Ronald P. Formisano, *The Transformation of Political Culture: Massachusetts Parties, 1790s–1840s* (New York: Oxford University Press, 1983), 287–88.

23. Lawrence B. Goodheart, *Abolitionist, Actuary, Atheist: Elizur Wright and the Reform Impulse* (Kent, Ohio: Kent State University Press, 1990), 105.

24. Quoted in Johnson, "Liberty Party in Massachusetts," 239. Also see Debra Gold Hansen, *Strained Sisterhood: Gender and Class in the Boston Female Anti-slavery Society* (Amherst: University of Massachusetts Press, 1993).

25. Quoted in Mary Fuhrer, " 'We all have something to do in the cause of freeing the

slave': The Abolition Work of Mary White" (paper presented at the Dublin Seminar, Deerfield, Mass., June 15–17, 2001), 13.

26. Charles H. Wesley, "The Participation of Negroes in Anti-Slavery Political Parties" (paper presented at the Annual Meeting of the Association for the Study of Negro Life and History, Columbus, Ohio, 1941), rptd. in McKivigan, *Abolitionism in American Politics and Government,* 160–202, esp. 167–68. Also Benjamin Quarles, *Black Abolitionists* (New York: Oxford University Press, 1969), 183–88.

27. *Minutes of the National Convention of Colored Citizens, held at Buffalo . . . August, 1843,* in Howard Hold Bell, ed., *Proceedings of the National Negro Conventions, 1830–1864* (New York: Arno Press, 1969).

28. Wesley, "Participation of Negroes in Anti-Slavery Political Parties," 172–73.

29. James O. Horton and Lois E. Horton, *Black Bostonians: Family and Community Struggle in Antebellum Boston* (New York: Holmes and Meier, 1979), 48–49. On Morris, see Laurie, *Beyond Garrison,* 247 ff.

30. Wesley, "Participation of Negroes in Anti-Slavery Political Parties," 176–78.

31. Ibid., 173. Also Quarles, *Black Abolitionists,* 183–88.

32. Johnson, "Liberty Party in Massachusetts," 242–44, and Laurie, *Beyond Garrison,* 49–76.

33. Laurie, *Beyond Garrison,* 76–80.

34. Ibid., 76–77.

35. John Greenleaf Whittier, *The Stranger in Lowell* (Boston: Waite, Pierce, 1845), 49.

36. Patrick Crim, " 'The Ballot Boxes Are Our Arms!' The Latimer Slave Case and the Liberty Party in Massachusetts" (seminar paper, University of Massachusetts Amherst, 1999), and Laurie, *Beyond Garrison,* 78–80.

37. Crim, "Ballot Boxes," 9. Also Vincent Y. Bowditch, *Life and Correspondence of Henry Ingersoll Bowditch,* 2 vols. (Boston: Houghton, Mifflin, 1902), 1:133–36.

38. (Boston) *Liberator,* Nov. 25, 1842. Hereafter *Lib.*

39. Ibid., Nov. 11, 1842.

40. Ibid., Jan. 17, 1843.

41. (Boston) *Emancipator,* Jan. 12, 19, and 26, 1843, and (Boston) *Daily Advertiser,* Dec. 1842–Jan. 1843, *passim.* Hereafter *Eman.* Also Arthur B. Darling, *Political Change in Massachusetts, 1824–1848: A Study of Liberal Movements in Politics* (New Haven: Yale University Press, 1925), 248–49.

42. *Lib.,* May 7, 1831. Also see Ruchames, "Race, Marriage, and Abolition in Massachusetts," and Dubow, "Not a Virtuous Woman."

43. *Eman.,* Dec. 1–8 and 29, 1842, and Jan. 12, 19, and 26, 1843. Also Darling, *Political Change in Massachusetts,* 248–49.

44. For a summary of the debate in the press, see Laurie, *Beyond Garrison,* 110–12. Also see Ruchames, "Race, Marriage and Abolition in Massachusetts," and Dubow, "Not a Virtuous Woman."

45. *Lib.,* June 4, 1834, Dec. 14, 1838, and Aug. 6, 1841. Also MASS, *Tenth Annual Report* (1842), 71–81.

46. *Lib.,* Oct. 15, 1841. Also ibid., Aug. 20, and Oct. 1–8 and 29, and Nov. 5, 1841.

47. MASS, *Twelfth Annual Report* (1844), 53.

48. *Eman.,* Mar. 30, 1843.

49. Dubow, "Not a Virtuous Woman," and Ruchames, "Jim Crow Railroads in Massachusetts."

50. Garrison to Henry Wright, Oct. 1, 1844, in Merrill, *Letters of William Lloyd Garrison,* 3:261–65. Quotation on 266.

51. Ibid., Garrison to Elizabeth Pease, Dec. 14, 1844, and Garrison to Richard Webb, Mar. 1, 1845, 273, 288.

52. This aspect of party activity is least well known. The work of Voss-Hubbard, "Slavery, Capitalism, and the Middling Sorts," suggests that the party was deeply engaged in local politics. I am assuming that it was at least one of the groups at work for the racial integration of town schools.

53. *Boston Courier,* Feb. 7, 1843.

54. Henry Wilson, *The Rise and Fall of the Slave Power in America,* 3 vols. (Boston: James R. Osgood, 1872–77), 1:495–98.

55. *Eman.,* Jan. 19 and Mar. 19–25, 1845. Also George A. Levesque, *Black Boston: African-American Life and Culture in Urban America, 1750–1860* (New York: Garland Publishing, 1994), 186–88.

56. Laurie, *Beyond Garrison,* 119–21. Also Mark Santow, "These Little Republican Temples: Race, Ethnicity, and Public Schooling in Antebellum Massachusetts" (seminar paper, University of Massachusetts Amherst, 1992), 7–9. Quotation on 10 in *Report of the Minority of the Committee of the Primary School Board on the Caste Schools of the City of Boston. . . . Doc. 23 1/2. Boston City Documents* (Boston: J. H. Eastburn, 1846).

57. Laurie, *Beyond Garrison,* 279–83.

58. Notable exceptions include Earle, *Jacksonian Antislavery,* esp. 123–43, and Eric Foner, "Racial Attitudes of the New York Free Soilers," in Foner, *Politics and Ideology in the Age of the Civil War* (New York: Oxford University Press, 1980), 77–93. For more traditional views, see Leslie M. Harris, *In the Shadow of Slavery: African Americans in New York City, 1626–1863* (Chicago: University of Chicago Press, 2003), and Volpe, *Forlorn Hope of Freedom.*

59. See esp. the illuminating portraits of David Wilmot and Gamaliel Bailey in Earle, *Jacksonian Antislavery,* 123–43, 145–47.

5

God, Garrison, and the Coming of the Civil War

JAMES BREWER STEWART

The historical sociologist Max Weber coined a term that captures the spiritual iconoclasm of William Lloyd Garrison. That term is *religious virtuoso*. According to Weber, religious virtuosos vividly sense God's immediate presence in their daily lives, and they open their hearts to the fresh revelations the Almighty chooses to impart to them. Inspired by these sudden illuminations, they stride confidently into the public arena demanding "moral revolutions," that is, spiritual transformations inspired by the Holy Spirit that will bring all human relationships into harmony with the will of the Lord.*

Religious virtuosos deeply oppose what they take to be worn-out dogmas, oppressive customs, and bankrupt traditions. Scorning the prevailing order, they condemn governments, churches, and "respectable" society for mocking God's revealed truths. As they do so, they often attempt to invent revolutionary alternatives. Garrison's contemporaries Joseph Smith, William Miller, and Alexander Campbell, for example, founded new religions. John Humphrey

*An earlier version of this chapter was delivered as a presidential address to the Society for Historians of the Early American Republic on July 24, 2005, at the Chemical Heritage Foundation in Philadelphia, and later published with the title "Reconsidering the Abolitionists in an Age of Fundamentalist Politics," *Journal of the Early Republic* 26, no. 1 (Spring 2006): 1–25. It is reprinted here with some amendment with the *Journal*'s permission.

Noyes and Adin Ballou embraced visions of heaven on earth and organized utopian communities. Still others, such as the Shakers, sought collective sanctification by withdrawing into adoptive families far from the fallen world.[1]

For Garrison, the virtuoso's calling developed as a journey into "universal Christian reform." In this journey he found himself guided by ongoing revelations. His revolutionary alternatives to established institutions became his newspaper, the *Liberator,* the New England Anti-Slavery Society and the American Antislavery Society, all of which supplied his personal and ideological moorings from 1833 to 1865.

Garrison's first illumination came in 1831 when he demanded immediate emancipation and declared himself a spokesman for "all mankind." Illumination expanded in the later 1830s when he rejected the literal truth of scripture, condemned the nation's churches as bastions of slavery, embraced Christian nonresistance, and insisted that God had created women and men no less than people of differing complexions as absolute equals. Illumination came to full fruition in 1842, when he advocated the peaceful dissolution of the Union between the North and the South, denounced the United States Constitution as "an agreement with hell," and insisted that those who voted in elections committed the gravest of sins. Garrison's fullest vision was as sweeping as it was radical, so rich a mixture of extremism that by 1840 many of his fellow abolitionists had recoiled in dismay from his leadership.[2]

A question immediately presents itself: Apart from making his name a scandal, what possible role could this ideologically marginal utopian have played in year-to-year northern politics between 1831 and 1861 as sectional division drove the nation to Civil War? How could someone so defiant of so much conventional wisdom have possibly influenced the northern electorate, those millions of ordinary men who cherished all that Garrison so bitterly condemned — their belief in white supremacy, their sense of "masculine superiority," their deep devotion to the federal Union, and their incessant involvement in party politics?

Asking this specific question about Garrison leads to a larger question still: What actual impact did the abolitionist movement itself, the very movement Garrison did so much to promulgate and influence, have in shaping the political crisis that led to the Civil War? In political terms, within the Free States, did the thirty years of agitation by the abolitionists really make a difference?

Answers to these questions begin with the recognition that a great many Protestant Americans, not just religious virtuosos like Garrison, strove to remake the nation to reflect the will of God. The era that scholars often refer to as "the Jacksonian Era" or the "Era of the Market Revolution" can just as accurately be termed the Era of Bible Politics. People in the antebellum era quarreled incessantly over the same overarching question that the abolitionists provoked — whether or not their nation ought to be refashioned as a "Christian Republic."

If you believed so, then (depending on chronology) the Sunday U.S. mail, the religion of Mormonism, and the issuance of liquor licenses must be prohibited. Masons must abolish their lodges. Catholic conspiracies must be exposed. The Cherokee and other acculturated Indians must never be removed. Those complicit with chattel slavery must embrace "immediate emancipation" or, far more commonly, the promise of colonization.

If you lived in the North, if these injunctions repelled you, if you feared for the continuing separation of church from state, the Democratic Party beckoned. If they reinforced your conviction that Christian principle secured the nation's freedom you likely favored the Whigs. But whichever your choice, the restless evangelicalism that continuously thrust these issues into politics was easy to identify.

Like it or not, evangelicalism entwined itself in politics because of the activism it empowered, the morally engaged laity it inspired, the energetic voluntary associations it underwrote, and the bitter contention it provoked over its vision of a godly republic. And during the 1830s, throughout the North, it became clear that many evangelicals "voted as they prayed, and prayed as they voted."

Abolitionists always had more in common with these pious Free State voters than may be apparent at first. Nearly every immediatist shared the evangelicals' fears that not only slavery but Masonry, Mormonism, Catholicism, freethinkers, Indian killers, immigrants, and liquor distillers threatened the nation's Christian foundations. Like most orthodox evangelicals, nearly every abolitionist believed that the "influence" of women should be mobilized in support of moral reforms. As a result, significant political relationships developed between these two groups during the antebellum decades. Yet all the while evangelicals continued to decry the abolitionists' religious "heresies" and to turn a cold shoulder to their pleas for emancipation. Few wholehearted converts to the abolitionist cause ever stepped forward from the ranks of those who "voted as they prayed and prayed as they voted."[3]

The complex political position of the abolitionists within the North becomes clearer if we evaluate it in relation to politicized evangelicalism of recent times. As historians, what do we make of antebellum religious activists such as Garrison while membership in fundamentalist churches mushrooms and evangelical voters helped in 2004 to reelect a self-proclaimed born-again president? Politicians with 90 percent positive ratings from the Christian Coalition have shaped policy on subjects ranging from stem cell research to

foreign affairs. With a fervor matching that of the civil rights movement of the
1960s, politicized evangelical activists against abortion and human trafficking
have claimed Garrison's mantle and also, thanks to the film *Amazing Grace,*
that of the British immediatist William Wilberforce by declaring themselves to
be the new abolitionists. And while public education retrenches, Bible-based
academies flourish. If you embrace these developments, the Republican Party
beckons. If they repel you, you're either a Democrat or you're alienated or
you're both. But if you are a Democrat who recognizes that evangelicals exercise inspired leadership in efforts to combat genocide, AIDS, and contemporary slavery, you're ambivalent. In any case, our age of Bible politics is a time,
if ever there was one, when historians seeking to understand the abolitionists'
roles in politics ought to take religion seriously.

Today's activists of the religious right have exercised political agency by
addressing what they identify as the most compelling moral questions of our
time. For whatever reasons, millions of voters and many influential politicians
have responded favorably in recent elections, and politics itself is changed.
Candidates have been elected, and laws have been passed. The proof of evangelicals having exercised political agency has been and continues to be these
tangible political results. Since radical opposition to slavery generated so
many of the most compelling moral questions of the antebellum age, one
might then ask, as I do in this chapter, this question: Given its obvious marginality, what political leverage, if any, did the abolitionist movement in any of its
pro- or anti-Garrisonian varieties exercise as the nation moved closer to Civil
War?

Political history yields largely negative answers. Historians do grant that
slaveholders overreacted to the abolitionists (Garrison most prominently) by
defending their institution all the harder. But this seems the opposite of agency.
Garrison's goal and that of all abolitionists was, after all, to see slavery elimi-
nated, not more strenuously defended. Historians who weigh the importance
of nativism, temperance, and free soil republicanism in the political realignment of the 1850s cite no reasons to emphasize the importance of any of the
abolitionists. Not Garrison and his followers. Not immediatist detractors
either.

Historians of ideology who distinguish between racist northern politicians
opposed to an expanding "slave power" and egalitarian activists seeking an
end to slavery do highlight the abolitionists, but only to underline their political marginality. For these scholars, Abraham Lincoln's denial of slavery's extension, not Garrison's calls for emancipation through "moral revolution,"
defined the Republicans' position. There are, to be sure, historians who continue to follow Gilbert Hobbes Barnes's notion of abolitionism's "broadening

impulse" by tracing antislavery politics in the 1840s and 1850s to immediatist origins. But even these scholars leave the abolitionists as a *movement* behind once their examinations move into the mid-1840s, when most of the anti-Garrisonian Liberty Party abolitionists merged with the Free Soilers.[4]

Are the many scholars who are creating today's renaissance in abolitionist studies concerned about their subjects' apparent irrelevance to political historians? Does it matter to them that no one representing the North in the halls of power seemed to have been responding directly to any of the immediate abolitionists, let alone to the spiritually untethered Garrison? Apparently not.

Instead, these scholars explain the abolitionists' agency without reference to a demonstrable capacity to shape formal politics. Such disinterest in tangible political results would hardly satisfy the antiabortion leaders of Operation Rescue. Yet it does lead historians of the abolitionists to emphasize two other forms of agency, each very important in its own right. Agency constitutes, first, the personally empowering insights, motivations, and self-understandings that abolitionists drew from participating in their visionary causes, precisely the sorts of illuminations that ignited and sustained the crusading vitality of Garrison and his fellow virtuosos. It involves, second, the crucial ideological process of projecting dissenting convictions directly into an otherwise racist and proslavery public sphere, a commitment to self-expression that permanently engaged Garrison from the moment he first announced in 1831, "Urge me not to moderation in a cause like the present. I am in earnest—I will not equivocate—I will not excuse—I will not retreat an inch—and I WILL BE HEARD!"[5]

As a result, the current renaissance of abolitionist scholarship has deeply illuminated the abolitionist movement's beliefs, strategies, tactics, and cultural productions. But it has not demonstrated its wider political impact. It has brilliantly charted the work of its contending factions and the ideas, arguments, and projects of its African American and its female participants. It has given us deep understandings of Garrison and his supporters and of the many abolitionists with whom he was at first united, but who later rejected his leadership. But it has not explained how the interventions of any of these groups might actually have changed northern politics.[6]

In short, we seem to be left with questions like these: What did all that agitation by all those abolitionists for all of those years finally amount to within the Free States—all those speeches, conventions, novels, narratives, newspapers, petitions, woodcuts, banners, and handbills? Did those in power representing the North and the voters who put them there take the abolitionists seriously enough to respond with something other than hostile indifference?

Abolitionist scholarship usually answers yes, but only by claiming in the most general way that the movement must have made a difference — somehow. But when political historians press these questions by asking for specifics, their findings render an unambiguous no. The indexes of Michael Morrison's and William Gineapp's recent accounts of sectional politics and the coming of the Civil War contain no entries for the abolitionists. Michael Holt's twelve-hundred-page *Rise and Fall of the Whig Party* gives as much attention in its index to the subject of "redistricting in Alabama" as to the "abolitionist movement."[7]

The point is not that either abolitionist studies or political history is right or wrong. Instead it is to observe that the two fields have lost contact with each other. To read in them simultaneously is to slip back and forth between alternate universes. So it seems worthwhile to work against historiographical fragmentation by considering the moral challenges posed by Garrison and his fellow crusaders as ones that extended directly into northern politics. I want to return here to the theme of Bible politics and to the opportunity that the current fundamentalist-driven moment gives us to take religion seriously. Along the way we may discover that abolitionists of all persuasions, Garrisonians and anti-Garrisonians alike, did exercise important agency in two-party politics within the Free States, but that they did so in ways that have eluded historians and that bear little resemblance to today's born-again activists.

Just how radically different in theology were Garrison and his coworkers from most of today's conservative evangelicals? From the 1830s up to the Civil War, most black and white abolitionists shared Garrison's postmillennial vision of their Christian lives and duties. Abolitionists, above all, understood Christ as a closely abiding earthly presence with all who receive. Guided by His inspiration, redeemed Christians work with Him to bring the world into harmony with God's designs — freeing the South's slaves, in this instance.[8]

Today, in sharpest contrast, most Protestant fundamentalists typically embrace premillennialism. In this vision, Christ will return to reign as prophesied only after the world has undergone terrible tribulation — the rule of the Antichrist and the redemptive separation of the saved from the damned. In the meantime, Christians must live out in politics their conformity to literalist understandings of scripture. They must oppose gay rights, abortion, evolution, and so forth while advocating the world over for those who share their creeds.[9]

Both visions contain compelling critiques of society's ills. Both express encompassing desires to endow life with sacred meanings and redemptive experiences. Both convey energizing calls for individual activism. Both make fervent appeals to an angry God. Both place highest premium on moral suasion to convert others. But these similarities, which are common to many religious movements besides evangelical Protestantism, end here.

The abolitionists' overall vision offers extraordinarily hopeful, even utopian views of our capacities to steer the future toward God's intended goals. Therefore, as many historians have emphasized, the movement was profoundly antiauthoritarian, and its most creative members truly were religious virtuosos. As they improvised still more expansive ways of enacting God's will in everyday life, they shattered religious orthodoxies time and again, a process perfectly illustrated beginning in the late 1830s by Garrison's ever-expanding commitments to an ever-larger number of spiritually driven causes—women's rights, anticlericalism, nonresistance, nonvoting, and peaceful disunion.[10]

By contrast, today's fundamentalist activists can seem profoundly pessimistic to those outside their circle. In their own hearts and minds, however, theirs, too, is a faith of unconquerable hope. Though there's nothing we sin-plagued people can do to arrest the future's spiral into perdition, redemption will prevail with Christ's Second Coming. In the meantime biblically sanctioned literalism determines the conduct of the saved in families, in churches, in the workplace, in voluntary associations, and in one's political choices. Highly motivated religious activists abound. Spiritual originality and iconoclasm such as Garrison's do not. Obedience rules, not "virtuosity." Authority inspires, not spontaneity.[11]

This contrast becomes all the more persuasive when developed in antebellum historical contexts. Only in the region most hostile to Garrison specifically and to all that the abolitionists stood for generally, the lower South, can one find a pre–Civil War parallel to the politicized religious authoritarianism so common in the early twenty-first century. As Stephanie McCurry and Christine Heyerman have both demonstrated, the explosion of evangelical revivalism that swept through that region on the eve of secession affirmed as sacred the very same patriarchal prerogatives Garrison most vocally denounced: the rights of white yeomen and planters to rule over their putative dependents. The South's demands were for continuing subjugation of slaves and women and for secession, not for the generalized Christian liberation for which all immediatists stood. Its methods included seizing control of state and local politics and encouraging the forcible silencing of dissenters. The gulf between this variety of evangelical politics and the religious values espoused by the abolitionists could hardly be wider.[12]

This summary, then, makes two suggestions. The first is that contemporary fundamentalists ought to think again, hard, before claiming the abolitionists as their historical ancestors. Standards of historical accuracy confirm such claims as specious. The second is that today's religious right finds political agency a straightforward exercise. For abolitionists, such was never the case. Obedient to established authority, fundamentalist activists today embrace prevailing governance in order to conform it to God's will by mobilizing voters, winning elections, discouraging dissent, and passing laws. Garrison and his supporters, by contrast, found themselves by 1840 so alienated from all conventional politics that they denounced the federal Constitution and urged the boycotting of elections. Equally disillusioned, many of his abolitionist opponents found themselves driven to launch their own emancipationist Liberty Party.

Why? In general, it was because conventional American political values seemed to these anti-institutional Christians to be ever more deeply mired in unholy coercion and expedience. But more specifically it was also because abolitionists concluded in the later 1830s that governance on all levels and both major political parties, Whig and Democratic alike, were united in their implacable hostility to immediate emancipation.

For this basic reason, the political consequences of the abolitionists' demand for abolishing slavery and of equivalent demands today for, say, outlawing abortion are stunningly unalike. Antiabortion activists automatically generate immense political partisanship in response to their agitation. This is precisely what today's parties thrive on in order to compete against each other, build centers of power, and forward legislative agendas. As pro-choice Democrats contend against anti-choice Republicans, political agency multiplies with rallies, campaign contributions, blogs, electronic petitions, and voting. Women and people of color in all parts of the country participate on all sides.

The contrast between this contemporary dynamic and the situation facing the abolitionist movement during the 1830s could not be more obvious. The women and the African Americans who responded to Garrison's initial appeals utterly defied exceptionally potent norms of white racism and male supremacy simply by attempting to participate in their own movement. Meanwhile, during this same period, the movement itself united around a full-throated demand for the instant liberation of the nation's second largest capital investment: three million enslaved members of a despised race. Little wonder that this exceptionally subversive and potentially explosive crusade did not prompt competitive divisions pro and con between national parties in the 1830s similar to those generated by fundamentalist activism today. Instead it provoked enormous opposition from nearly all sectors of white society.

The horrifying results were measured throughout the 1830s by the literal reign of terror visited on the abolitionists—by gag rules passed, mailbags ransacked, printing presses vandalized, suspected slave rebels executed, "colored schools" mobbed, northern black neighborhoods reduced to ashes, and abolitionists denounced from pulpits. The South Carolina State Legislature debated a resolution offering five thousand dollars for the delivery of Garrison's head and ten thousand for "the whole man." All this is certainly a far remove from the positions of political power, financial comfort, and personal security enjoyed today by right-wing spiritual/political leaders such as Gary Bauer, Paul Weyrich, and James Dobson.[13]

As abolitionists weathered the terrors of the 1830s what of that influential sector of the northern electorate that was voting as it prayed and praying as it voted? As Richard Carwardine and Daniel Walker Howe have shown, these evangelical voters held religious and social values that gave them much in common with the abolitionists. Both groups entertained postmillennial visions that fired their activism and directed their voluntary associations. As already noted, both groups charged Masons, Catholics, liquor distillers, freethinkers and Indian removers as well as slaveholders with sponsoring godless immorality. Both relied heavily on "female influence" and the day-to-day work of women to forward their religious causes.[14]

So great were the commonalities between these two groups that the abolitionists at first expected the northern evangelicals to flock to their crusade. But for all their piety, these were not religious virtuosos. When it came to politics, they prized well-organized moral renovation, not the impulse of moral revolution. Their opposition to slavery led them to colonization or to tortured hand wringing but certainly not to immediatism. Their devotion to scripture left them appalled by Garrisonian heresies and willing to expel abolitionists of every persuasion from their churches. Sharing much with the abolitionists culturally and politically but deeply fearful of religious extremism, immediatism, and the threat of racial equality, they headed in droves into the Whigs, the party that appealed to their full range of moral and spiritual concerns.[15]

By 1840, their migration was complete. Many northern evangelical voters now fused their opposition to slavery with a still broader opposition to everything for which the secular Jacksonians were alleged to have stood. While log cabins and hard cider attracted workaday laborers and artisans, Whig Bible politics spoke powerfully to spiritually "uplifted" northerners who voted as they prayed and prayed as they voted. Reflecting on this trend the immediatist Henry B. Stanton reported ruefully during the elections of 1840, "49/50ths of our friends are determined to wade to their armpits in molten lava to drive Van Buren from power." Without any apparent sense of inconsistency, such evangelicals rallied behind the slaveholding William Henry Harrison for president in 1840, not the abolitionist candidate James G. Birney, who received a scant seven thousand votes.[16]

As the presidential election proceeded, disagreement deepened within the abolitionist movement. Spurred by the realization that an overwhelming national majority scorned their appeals, they commenced an intense inquiry into the question of what new truths their trials by violence were revealing and what, as a consequence, the Lord now required. Their deeply conflicting answers yielded new and immensely creative approaches to politics, and in this divisive process Garrison's influence predominated.

Garrison was at least as aghast as other immediatists at the nation's hostile response to their movement. "When we first unfurled the banner of *The Liberator*," he exclaimed in 1837, "we did not anticipate that, in order to protect southern slavery, the Free States would voluntarily trample under foot all order, law and government, or brand the advocates of universal liberty as incendiaries." In his opinion, such repression laid bare the utter corruptness of organized religion, secular government, and even relationships between ordinary people. Sin so deeply entrenched and so all-encompassing could, he announced, be overcome only if abolitionists embraced Christian perfectionism, rejected all forms of coercion, practiced nonresistance, and refused to collaborate with God-defying authority. It was an illumination that quickly led him to women's rights, election boycotts, anticlericalism, and calls to dissolve the federal Union.[17]

As Garrison grew increasingly radical, he, his supporters, and his ever more numerous critics quarreled and conspired against one another. By 1840 the movement had permanently split into fiercely competing factions, all with entirely novel approaches to politics. Garrisonians, for example, followed Abbey Kelley Foster, Angelina Grimké, and Sarah Grimké by explicitly linking God's will and slave emancipation with women's rights. They also insisted that abolitionists must sever their spiritual ties to the slave-ridden government and publicly abstain from casting ballots. Some of Garrison's leading opponents developed an entirely contrary but no less novel approach, the Liberty Party, a third political party designed to inspire the northern electorate to vote for "immediate emancipation." Though individual black activists could be counted in each abolitionist faction they, too, struck out in important new political directions. Responding to their white colleagues' distractions, they began reinvigorating their own independent organizations to fight for their own equality by openly challenging segregation and racist restrictions on their right to vote. In short, abolitionists of all persuasions now began acting as political no less than religious virtuosos. This, in turn, began involving them with the northern Whig Party.[18]

To understand how this process unfolded, let us once more contrast antebellum Bible politics with Bible politics today. Two points stand out. First, today's conservative evangelicals have become active Republicans in order to bend the party to their demands. Back in the 1830s and 1840s, abolitionists could not have cared less about controlling any political party, Whigs included. Instead, as "passionate outsiders" (to borrow John Stauffer's felicitous term) they worked to morally transform the entire political system to accord with Christ's teachings, not to turn themselves into an existing party's electoral base. Once more, the differences between a William Lloyd Garrison and, say, a Pat Robertson could hardly be clearer.[19]

Second and just as important, the antebellum Whig Party and today's Republican Party display entirely different structures. As a result, their responses to religious activism could not be less alike. Conservative Republican strategists today pitch to their evangelical base by demanding their party's purity on questions such as abortion and gay rights. Conformity defines and mobilizes political loyalty. Whigs, in starkest contrast, agreed to disagree about slavery during the 1840s. A decentralized party structure encouraged precisely such regional variation. In the South, Whigs spoke as slavery's avid protectors. In the Free States they criticized slavery, advocated "northern rights," and sometimes defended the abolitionists. Why? Because this was a highly effective way for Whigs to win elections in both sections: they espoused economic nationalism while presenting their party as a compelling regional alternative to the Democrats on slavery questions. "From its birth," Michael Holt reminds us, "the Whig party could and did survive a fundamental division on the slavery question." Similarly, a post–World War II Democratic Party bent on preserving New Deal liberalism found room for segregationists like Richard Russell and for African American militants like Adam Clayton Powell.[20]

As the 1840s opened, the political situation confronting the abolitionists looked something like this: Agreeing across the Mason-Dixon line to disagree about slavery, pious Whigs fastened on the Democrats as their crucial negative reference group: a "Bible politician's" rogues' gallery of liquor peddlers, gamblers, Catholics, antievangelicals, freethinkers, Indian killers, duelists, slave drivers, stockjobbers, and so forth. In the Free States, however, there was also a significant affirmative reference group for Whigs to interact with as they battled the Democrats: the abolitionists.

Affinities originated in the evangelical religious culture shared by the two groups. Affinities blossomed in the Bible politics constituencies for whose attentions both groups competed. Northern Whigs knew that victory over the Democrats depended on retaining the support of these important evangelical voters, especially when the possibility of Texas annexation and war with Mexico raised the issue of slavery's expansion. Whatever their convictions regarding the "sin of slavery," northern Whig leaders feared that abolitionist opposition would work to the advantage of the Democrats by drawing their evangelical supporters away to the Liberty Party in 1844 and to the Free Soil Party in 1848. Firm ideological distinctions between Whigs and abolitionists began to blur as often as they sharpened as they battled against each other for the support of northern evangelicals. As Stanley Elkins correctly explained so long ago, antislavery Whigs were now becoming not the abolitionists' formal converts but instead their ideologically more moderate "fellow travelers."[21]

Beautifully crafted state and regional studies with which we are well familiar show exactly where these Whig/abolitionist codependencies flourished. Together these locations constituted a northern Bible belt where abolitionist political agency rooted itself — Ohio's Western Reserve and Firelands Districts — New York State's Burnt Over District — Indiana's Burnt District — Lower Michigan's southeastern and central counties — Massachusetts's western counties as well as its manufacturing and coastal towns — districts in Vermont surrounding Montpellier — New Hampshire villages and farmsteads outside of Dover and Concord — and small towns scattered across southern Maine. Together these regions constituted a broad band of deep evangelical belief, vibrant social activism, and Whig loyalty that spanned the Free States from the Atlantic to the Mississippi.

In all of these places canals, turnpikes, toll roads, and waterborne shipping fostered cash crop agriculture, commercial enterprise, artisan production, and urban markets. Proliferating newspapers created sophisticated networks of communication that ensured citizens' heightened involvement in national affairs. So did large concentrations of public schools, private academies, and voluntary associations led by women as well as by men. In short, the social and economic character of these regions harmonized perfectly with Whig promises of internal improvements, high tariffs, reliable banking, evangelical values, and "moral uplift." Voters in these strongholds of piety exercised a potent influence over the fate of the party at election time, and Whig politicians did all they could to energize this vital electoral base.[22]

In this context Whigs and abolitionists became increasingly involved with one another once religious virtuosos turned their hands to local Bible politics. Here, politically, is where all those speeches, conventions, narratives, newspapers, petitions, woodcuts, racial uplift projects, banners, and handbills had their greatest significance. Here also is where black and female abolitionist activists exercised their most immediate political impact. Maintaining annual cycles of repeating activism, abolitionists created rich local environments of radical opposition to slavery that no Whig politician in the North's Bible belt could safely ignore.

While Whigs rolled up majorities, charismatic Garrisonian "headliners" like Abby Kelley Foster, Wendell Phillips, and Garrison himself energized the faithful by keynoting annual meetings, condemning voting, challenging the Liberty Party, and calling Whig politicians to account. Liberty Party activists founded newspapers, recruited competitive candidates, and sharply contrasted their "practical" approaches to politics with Garrisonian "ultraism." They built alliances with evangelical congregations involving women as well as men. They perfected strategies designed to draw off Whig supporters. Abolitionist women of every abolitionist persuasion developed their roles further still when supplying day-to-day leadership in a multiplying succession of meetings, fairs, reading groups, and petition drives. Blacks redefined the politics of race by challenging discrimination, fugitive slave laws, and the moral standing of overbearing whites — overbearing white abolitionists and politicians included. As abolitionist politics intensified and local Whigs prepared for the next elections, the two groups treated each other as codependents so often do when quarreling over shared values and living space, that is, with a volatile mixture of enablement and abuse.[23]

On the enabling side of the equation the two groups applied the fellow traveler principle in the 1840s to collaborate on a number of abolitionist-initiated campaigns. A listing of these reveals just how often northern Whigs acted openly as the abolitionists' allies. In Massachusetts, "conscience" Whigs supported the struggles of black and white activists that overturned antimiscegenation laws, school segregation, and segregation of public transportation. In New York State, Ohio, Pennsylvania, and Michigan, Whigs campaigned in favor of personal liberty laws and for unsuccessful efforts by African American abolitionists to repeal restrictions on suffrage. (Little wonder that enfranchised African Americans voted overwhelmingly Whig!) And in the U.S. Congress, as we all know, it was Whig representatives from Bible belt districts who most persistently put forward antislavery petitions (including those from women and blacks); who most disruptively protested against the gag rule, the internal slave trade, and slavery in the District of Columbia; and who most stridently protested against slavery's expansion.[24]

On the abusive end of this relationship each side exploited the other shamelessly in order to amplify the political impact of its opposition to slavery. Abolitionists of every persuasion excoriated Whigs as hypocrites for supporting slaveholding candidates. Regardless of faction they called on voters to disdain this "slave-ridden" party. Vote instead for true Bible politics, urged the Liberty Party's advocates, that is, for candidates pledged to immediate emancipation. Spurn that "covenant with death," the U.S. Constitution, responded the Garrisonians. Obey the Christian imperative to spurn all evil. Do not vote at all.

In this heated disagreement, as Bruce Laurie's chapter in this book makes clear, Garrisonian disunionists and third-party abolitionists played quite distinct political roles. In the practical business of influencing election results and shaping legislation, Liberty Party activists proved the more effective politicians, a fact that Garrisonians themselves grudgingly acknowledged. Admitted Garrison's politically astute friend and collaborator, the rhetorically gifted Phillips, "As fast as we . . . make abolitionists, the new converts run right to the Liberty Party. . . . It is disheartening to see that every blow we strike falls in some degree against ourselves." As Phillips realized, the more compellingly he and his fellow Garrisonians spoke against the "proslavery" Union and condemned political parties, the less willing antislavery voters were likely to be to forfeit their franchise and the more likely they would be to vote for the first available Liberty Party or Free Soil candidate. Despite their quite contrary intentions, Garrisonian agitation had the effect of stimulating votes for third parties opposed to slavery, for, as Phillips correctly observed, "an American idolizes the ballot box."[25]

Whigs, for their part, had reasons aplenty for replying very harshly to their abolitionist critics as they sought to prevent critical defections to antislavery third parties. They took strong antislavery positions and appealed to pious voters to reject "one idea-ed abolitionism," whether Liberty Party or Garrisonian, as a gross impracticality. They lashed out particularly hard against third-party activists as tools of the slave-ridden Jacksonians. But whatever the indictment, whoever the target, abolitionists expanded their political agency whenever they inspired northern Whigs to campaign with heightened urgency against slavery.

The extent to which northern Whigs engaged in this fellow traveling out of high moral conviction instead of cold calculation can never be measured. Clearly there was a mixture of both. William H. Seward, who knew the "Burnt Over District" as well as anyone, sensed the vitality of moral principles when writing of proposals for Texas annexation. "The reckless folly of the Administration and the unprincipled adoption of it by our opponents have loosed our tongue stays," he concluded. "Slavery is henceforth and forever one of the elements of political action in the republic. The ground the public mind has traveled cannot be retraced."[26]

The thoughts of one high-ranking Whig politician, however, make plain that calculation should never be underestimated. In the heat of the presidential campaign of 1844 this strategist, James A. Briggs, chair of the Ohio Whig Central Committee, advised as follows in a confidential letter: Congressman Joshua Giddings from the Western Reserve portion of the Bible belt must be supported in his reelection bid and encouraged to speak his full mind on questions of slavery when campaigning across the state for Henry Clay. This, Briggs well knew, was the same Giddings who defended the rights of slaves to rise against their masters; who ferociously defied the gag rule; whose daughters proudly counted themselves as Garrisonian feminists; who, himself, much enjoyed sharing speakers' platforms with leading Garrisonians; who openly aided fugitives; and who rose in the House at the slightest provocation to condemn slaveholding as a moral abomination: "It would give us the abolitionist vote of the district," Briggs explained, "and exert a good influence throughout the state by out trumping the [abolitionist] third party ultras. . . . Whigs make no sacrifice of principle or measure as Mr. G. is a Whig . . . who will do us most good on the stump."[27]

As Briggs's remarks make clear, dedicated abolitionists active in the Whigs' evangelical base were now exerting a substantial influence on his party. This, by any measure, amounted to political agency. But it is equally obvious that the strategy-conscious Briggs harbored no worries. As he saw it, unleashing the "firebrand" Giddings and others like him would neither divide his party along north/south lines nor jeopardize the institution of slavery.

To explain his confidence we need only recall the Whigs' continuing agreement to disagree about slavery issues. In 1844, Whigs both North and South had skirted the issue of slavery's expansion by opposing further territorial acquisitions. In 1848 southern Whigs claimed that Zachary Taylor despised the anti-extensionist Wilmot Proviso. If elected, he would successfully oppose it. Northern Whigs guaranteed that the moment Congress passed the proviso, Taylor would sign it.[28]

The strategy Briggs was recommending had important consequences for his party. In the short term, the more abolitionists engaged northern Whigs as fellow travelers and competed against them at the polls, the more deeply defined by antislavery the northern Whigs themselves became. The more intensely northern Whigs promoted antislavery to their evangelical base, the more effectively they campaigned against the Democrats. Throughout the 1840s, the vast majority of Free State evangelicals remained convinced that the Whig Party represented the full range of their moral concerns — concerns about temperance, banking, land policy, Catholicism, and immigration, just as always — but also their increasingly deep and urgent concern about slavery's place in the nation's future.

In this manner, northern Whigs presented their party to evangelicals as a bulwark of antislavery. It was a strategy that helped it elect General Taylor while also yielding impressive state-level victories. As Jonathan Earle makes clear, the Free Soil Party in 1848 triumphed more often in districts dominated by antislavery Democrats hostile to Bible politics than in the evangelical Whig Bible belt, where abolitionism flourished. To outward appearances, the antislavery stimulus supplied by the abolitionists actually helped make the Whig Party stronger. Little wonder that immediatists so bitterly criticized the Whigs for stealing their audiences and watering down their doctrines.[29]

Yet the Whigs' short-term strength led to deeper weakness. Scholars disagree about exactly what led to the party's collapse. Yet most do agree that the Whig Party faltered in the 1850s once it abruptly broke faith with its northern constituents on the many issues it had always championed. Slavery questions ranked high among these. When raw sectional conflict in Washington over slavery's expansion finally undermined the party's agreement to disagree across the Mason-Dixon line, northern Whig leaders implicated themselves in the compromises of 1850. To the dismay of their northern evangelical constituents, "doughfaced" Whigs now spoke for a party that suddenly supported a harsh new fugitive slave law, the suppression of abolitionist agitation, the possibility of slavery's extension into the Nevada Territories, and an end to all political discussions of slavery.

It amounted to a wrenching reversal of field. A decade of mutually reinforcing political agitation by abolitionists of every faction had led many evangelical northern Whigs to expect unshakable antislavery from their party — that was certainly what party leaders had encouraged them to believe. In the disturbing aftermath of the compromises, the lingering impact of abolitionist political agency could be felt as alarming numbers of disillusioned northern Whigs stayed home on election days.[30]

To be clear, powerful issues in addition to the party's shifting stance on slavery explain the Whigs' slow demise in the early 1850s. The northern Whig retreat from antislavery and the continuing impact of abolitionist political agency can only be partially credited with these results. As several historians have emphasized, Whigs suddenly began looking strikingly like Democrats on other crucial issues in addition to slavery. A wave of German immigrants representing a huge new pool of uncommitted voters induced Whig leaders to suppress their traditional opposition to alcohol, immigrants, and Catholics. A booming economy took the edge off such traditional Whig issues as tariff and banking reform. Many voters now discerned "not a dime's worth of difference" between Whigs and Democrats on any of the familiar issues. In the view of many evangelical northerners the "turncoat" Whigs had betrayed them, not just on the slavery question, but on every moral issue for which the party had always stood.[31]

As David Brion Davis and Leonard L. Richards have demonstrated, fears of conspiratorial subversion had always played a powerful role in shaping antebellum political ideologies. Now, in the early 1850s, these fears coalesced into a potent antiparty spirit. Northern evangelicals spurned the Whig Winfield Scott as president in 1852 while warning of unholy plotting that heavily implicated the slave power as well as Catholics, immigrants, and liquor dealers. Now that slavery questions had been banished by the two political parties, even a vote for the much-diminished Free Soilers was no longer a viable vote of conscience. Instead, it was a vote wasted. In 1844 and 1848, there had been clear antislavery options that had promised tangible political consequences to those who voted as they prayed — a choice between the Whigs and a competing third party.

By 1852, however, all such options had vanished. In these dismal times for abolitionists the only viewpoint vindicated seemed to be Garrison's, who had insisted all along that Heaven-provoking godlessness saturated American politics. The political outlets through which Bible belt evangelicals had always addressed the problem of slavery had now abruptly closed. In their place arose volatile feelings of antiparty frustration and mounting desires to express building resentment. Little wonder that the new Fugitive Slave Law proved all but unenforceable in Bible belt centers of Whig and abolitionist "codependency" and that Garrisonians increasingly adjusted their commitments to nonviolence to allow for resistance to "slave-catchers."[32]

All of which goes far to explain why *Uncle Tom's Cabin* attracted far more notice in 1852 than the Whig presidential candidate, Scott. Harriet Beecher Stowe captured perfectly the full indictment of slavery developed by northern evangelicals over more than a decade. It also offered an imaginative outlet for those who could no longer vote as they prayed but who also could not bring themselves to join with Garrison in disavowing the Constitution. Hers was a masterpiece of literary fellow traveling.

Quite likely Michael Holt is correct in concluding that after 1850 "most Americans" considered the question of slavery's extension "permanently settled" and that they "expected never to have to confront that divisive question again." If so, the popularity of Stowe's novel makes clear that many in the North found this expectation deeply disturbing and looked beyond voting for new ways to express their disapproval. Resisting the Fugitive Slave Law constituted one such approach, one eagerly adopted by even nonresistants such as Garrison, who were now beginning to exhibit increasingly conflicted attitudes toward the use of violence. Another was that taken by anticompromise Whigs, Democrats, and Free Soil leaders. In state legislatures they arranged political deals that brought powerful fellow travelers into the U.S. Senate: Charles Sumner, Benjamin Franklin Wade, Salmon P. Chase, and Henry Wilson. Stowe's readers, opponents of the Fugitive Slave Law, and politicians who created Senate seats for fellow travelers were all now approaching the two-party system as "passionate outsiders," much as Garrison had always urged, as steeped in corruption and ripe for transformation.[33]

The transformation, if that's what it was, began with the passage of the Kansas–Nebraska Act in 1854. Though antislavery ideology in the North now sustained itself independent of specific legislative enactments, the power to reignite open sectional conflicts remained in the hands of the politicians such as those who repealed the Missouri Compromise. Yet after more than a decade of voting as they prayed, a significant portion of the Free State electorate, its Bible belt evangelicals, had just undergone an election cycle unlike any other — one that had deepened their fears and sent them seeking new outlets for expressing their resentments. Now, with the repeal of the 1820 Compromise, they looked all the more to politicians who would forcefully oppose slavery. Their defunct Whig Party had always encouraged them to expect this. More basic still, this was what they believed Christian conscience required. This is what their "codependent" relationship with the abolitionist movement had been all about.

Commenting on the Republicans, the Liberty and Free Soil Party veteran Gamaliel Bailey observed in the mid-1850s that a "political party is not a church or a philanthropic association." I am not arguing here that the Republican Party came into being as a spontaneous expression of evangelical conscience and abolitionist agency. Far from it. As we know, the party of Lincoln was a coalition constructed from a welter of conflicting interests and ideologies that had little to do with the abolitionists. For example, historians continue to assess the importance of the fleetingly powerful Know-Nothing Party in destroying the Whigs, disarranging the Democrats, and shaping the emerging Republicans. We are, moreover, only now beginning to understand the important roles that northern Democrats played in antislavery politics and within the Republican Party. The political impact within the United States of slavery and postemancipation conflicts in the greater Atlantic world also needs further study. So do the political implications of the abolitionists' direct attacks on southern slavery, documented by Stanley Harrold. The most pressing and least understood questions of all involve the impact on party politics of northern women, the vast majority of whom had not the slightest connection to Garrisonian feminism; they intervened in Free State political culture decisively during the 1840s and 1850s through evangelical churches, moral reform organizations, literary productions, and female academies and colleges. But whatever the mix of factors and unanswered questions, it is clear that secular political managers and insiders, not religious virtuosos, presided over a Republican organization that had no incentive to collaborate with the likes of William Lloyd Garrison.[34]

Abolitionists of all persuasions quickly realized this. They complained bitterly about how far removed they found themselves from the new Republican mainstream. They lamented over how deeply infected the new party was with white supremacy and antiabolitionism. Republicans made every effort to ensure that this was precisely where the abolitionists would find themselves.

Charged by slaveholders and by northern Democrats that they, the Republicans, were themselves covert abolitionists and race "amalgamators," party leaders defended themselves by condemning the movement as vehemently as possible. Abolitionists suddenly found themselves playing the role of the Republicans' negative reference group, precisely the opposite role they had played in the politics of the northern Whigs. All remaining ties between the abolitionist movement and electoral politics disintegrated, and abolitionist political agency within the two-party system collapsed.[35]

In its absence, as the 1850s wore on, abolitionists pursued scattered and highly individualistic actions. Some, like Garrison, yearned to join the Republicans but with great ambivalence because they remained deeply troubled by the party's openly racist version of antislavery. The party practiced "feeble," "indefinite," "partial," and "one-sided" politics, he complained, even while admitting during the presidential elections of 1856, "If there were no moral barrier to our voting, and if we had a million votes to bestow, we would gladly give them all to the Republican Candidate." Some who normally were Garrison's strongest supporters, however, shared none of Garrison's divided mind and instead condemned the new party outright. Wendell Phillips, most of all, gained unique celebrity as the premiere radical emissary to the public at large by filling lecture halls across the Free States with audiences that cheered his charismatic calls to spurn the Republicans on behalf of freeing the slave.[36]

Countersubversion captured abolitionists' imaginations as never before, bringing them together across long-established factional and racial lines. Vigilance Committees led by Garrisonians and third-party abolitionists together styled themselves as latter-day minutemen and Sons of Liberty. Some religious virtuosos contemplated the "righteous violence" of slave insurrection, a vision that captured the imagination of Liberty men such as Gerrit Smith and Frederick Douglass no less than Garrisonian stalwarts like Phillips and Henry Clarke Wright. Still others dreamed of a truly emancipationist political party or explored the efficacy of compensated emancipation. African American abolitionists felt ever more closely drawn to black nationalism, weighed the pros and cons of emigration, and practiced armed resistance against slave catchers.

Times had changed profoundly for William Lloyd Garrison and for all the abolitionists since the 1840s. Back then, their deep and varied involvement in Bible politics had stimulated the North's two-party system to battle over the future of slavery and to question racial discrimination within the Free States. Now, stripped of their electoral pertinence, politics seemed to offer them nothing. So instead, they resisted, yearned, and conspired. Congress meantime lurched from crisis to crisis while fears of the slave power continued to deepen and spread. What more empowering an environment could John Brown have asked for? In this respect, the collapse of their political agency, not its exercise, led abolitionists inspired by righteous violence to play their most obvious and most disruptive roles in bringing on Civil War. Even the great pioneer of Christian nonresistance, Garrison himself, ultimately sensed his pacifism to be increasingly untenable. In the midst of the violence of the Kansas border wars he exclaimed that "there is not a drop of blood in my veins both as an abolitionist and as a peace man that does not flow with the northern tide of sentiment to defeat the barbaric and tyrannous slave power."[37]

Once more, the contrast between the abolitionists' confusion and marginalization and the political potency of twenty-first-century right wing evangelicals could not be more obvious. For all their complaints of religious oppression by secular society, contemporary conservative religious activists actually exercise enormous political agency at the highest levels of governance. Take, for instance, the United States Supreme Court. Here the influence of evangelical lobbying helped select and confirm the newest justices and the substance of what the Court is likely to decide. For the abolitionists during the 1850s, the equivalent of this right-wing influence would have been a historically unimaginable Supreme Court majority of militant fellow travelers, not the overtly racist and proslavery Roger B. Taney, deciding the case of *Dred Scott vs Sandford*. At the end of the 1850s, quite obviously, Garrison and his fellow abolitionists continued to face political circumstances utterly unlike those pertaining to today's religious right. The most pertinent historical connections to be drawn between modern conservative evangelicals and evangelicals during the antebellum era are confirmed, once again, to be the forces of proslavery, not of abolitionism.

In 1860 Phillips claimed far too much for abolitionist political agency in stating that his movement "gave these [Republicans] a cause to fight for and a platform to stand on. It put them in office. It gave them their votes." The better assessment was Bailey's caution that political parties should never be confused with churches. In no sense were the abolitionists directly responsible for the Republican vote in 1860. But Phillips's claim was not entirely unfounded. During the 1840s, the abolitionist movement had, indeed, given the northern Whig Party a "cause to fight for and a platform to stand on," and this, in turn, had held important consequences for the Republicans.[38]

In the Free State Bible belt, during the 1840s, a "great, silent army of abolitionists," Garrisonian and anti-Garrisonian alike, interacted constantly with evangelicals, who took their religion to heart, generally voted Whig, and placed opposition to slavery high among their many moral concerns. Always attentive to immediatist opposition, northern Whig politicians certainly did take the abolitionists' challenges utterly seriously. In closely contested campaigns against the Democrats, party leaders responded to abolitionists' political attacks by defining their party as an emphatically antislavery organization. Whig fellow travelers made distinctions between abolitionism and antislavery increasingly elusive. Codependent relationships with the abolitionists increased the Whigs' competitiveness. Party leaders responded to abolitionists' challenges by assuring evangelicals that voting Whig meant standing up to slavery. When the Whigs abruptly abandoned their guarantees, these evangelicals helped foster a political realignment that made unyielding opposition to slaveholders' claims a leading feature of the Republican Party. And finally, when the abolitionists' political agency ended after 1854, they directly threatened both slavery and the political process by transforming their movement into one that fostered countersubversion, confrontation, and violence.

In all these ways the movement so frequently and so profoundly shaped by William Lloyd Garrison possessed more than enough political agency to justify much fuller index entries in books that explain the politics of the coming of the Civil War. The abolitionists did not cause that conflict. They never came close to achieving the postmillennial vision that Garrison evoked so compellingly in the first issue of *The Liberator* — the Godly revolution that he prophesied would roll peacefully onward "till every chain be broken and every bondsman set free!" The fate of religious virtuosos is almost always disappointment. Yet in an age when so many voted as they prayed, the abolitionists' political activism led evangelicals to confirm that opposing slavery was a prime responsibility of Christian citizenship. That confirmation went far to ensure that as civil war drew closer, so did an ultimate reckoning with "the peculiar institution."[39]

Notes

1. See Max Weber, "The Social Psychology of World Religions," in H. H. Gerth and C. Wright Mills, eds. and translators, *From Max Weber: Essays on Sociology* (New York: Macmillan, 1946), 267–301, 323–59. Robert H. Abzug, *Cosmos Crumbling: American Reform and the Religious Imagination* (New York: Oxford University Press, 1994), 4, 6, 17, 31–33, 110, and *passim,* brilliantly develops Weber's idea in relation to antebellum reform movements prior to 1840. Here I extend this concept into the 1840s and 1850s by connecting it to the political history of this era.

2. Standard biographies of Garrison include John L. Thomas, *The Liberator, William Lloyd Garrison: A Biography* (Boston: Little, Brown, 1963); Walter M. Merrill, *"Against Wind and Tide": A Biography of William Lloyd Garrison* (Cambridge: Harvard University Press, 1963); James Brewer Stewart, *William Lloyd Garrison and the Challenge of Emancipation* (Arlington Heights, Ill.: Harlan Davidson, 1992); and Henry Mayer, *All on Fire: William Lloyd Garrison and the Abolition of Slavery* (New York: St. Martin's, 1998).

3. In developing the theme of praying and voting, I am indebted to the starting point

provided in John R. McKivigan, "Vote as You Pray and Pray as You Vote: Church-Oriented Abolitionism and Antislavery Politics," in *Crusaders and Compromisers: Essays on the Relationship of the Antislavery Struggle to the Antebellum Party System*, ed. Alan Kraut (Westport, Conn.: Greenwood Press, 1983), 179–204. On relationships between political issues, Yankee evangelical piety, and abolitionists' Whiggish opposition to these various forms of "immorality," see Bertram Wyatt-Brown, "Prelude to Abolitionism: Sabbatarian Politics and the Rise of the Second Party System," *Journal of American History* 58 (Sept. 1971): 316–41; Paul Johnson, *A Shopkeeper's Millennium: Society and Revivals in Rochester, New York, 1815–1837* (New York: Hill and Wang, 1978); Paul Goodman, *Towards a Christian Republic: Antimasonry and the Great Transition in New England, 1826–1836* (New York: Oxford University Press, 1988); Harry Watson, *Liberty and Power: The Politics of Jacksonian America* (New York, 1990) 55–57, 178–79, 180–82, 222–23; Abzug, *Cosmos Crumbling*, 30–128.

4. Michael F. Holt, *The Political Crisis of the 1850s* (New York: Wiley, 1978); John Ashworth, *Slavery, Capitalism and Politics in the Antebellum Republic*, vol. 1, *Commerce and Compromise, 1820–1850* (Cambridge: Cambridge University Press, 1995); David Potter, *The Impending Crisis, 1848–1861* (New York: Harper and Row, 1976); Eric Foner, *Free Soil, Free Labor, Free Men: The Ideology of the Republican Party before the Civil War* (New York: Oxford University Press, 1970); Nicole Etcheson, *Bleeding Kansas: Contested Liberty in the Civil War Era* (Lawrence: University Press of Kansas, 2004); Lary Gara, "Slavery and the 'Slave Power': A Crucial Distinction," *Civil War History* 15 (Mar. 1969): 4–18; Gilbert Hobbs Barnes, *The Antislavery Impulse, 1830–1844* (New York: Appleton-Century-Crofts, 1936), 191–97; Merton Dillon, *The Abolitionists: The Growth of a Dissenting Minority* (DeKalb: Northern Illinois University Press, 1974); Richard H. Sewell, *Ballots for Freedom: Antislavery Politics in the United States, 1837–1860* (New York: Oxford University Press, 1976).

5. *Liberator*, January 1, 1831.

6. Claims made in this paragraph and the two preceding it are reflected in any number of outstanding studies of abolitionism. A few illustrative titles among the many that might be cited include Patrick Rael, *Black Identity and Black Protest in the Antebellum North* (Chapel Hill: University of North Carolina Press, 2002); Julie Roy Jeffrey, *The Great Silent Army of Abolitionism: Ordinary Women in the Antislavery Movement* (Chapel Hill: University of North Carolina Press, 1998); James and Lois Horton, *In Hope of Liberty: Culture, Community and Protest among Northern Free Blacks, 1700–1860* (New York: Oxford University Press, 1997); Richard S. Newman, *The Transformation of American Abolitionism: Fighting Slavery in the Early Republic* (Chapel Hill: University of North Carolina Press, 2002); Lawrence J. Friedman, *Gregarious Saints: Self and Community in Abolitionism, 1830–1870* (Cambridge: Cambridge University Press, 1982); Jean Fagan-Yellin, *Women and Sisters: The Abolitionist Feminists and American Culture* (New Haven: Yale University Press, 1989).

7. Michael A. Morrison, *Slavery and the American West: The Eclipse of Manifest Destiny and the Coming of the Civil War* (Chapel Hill: University of North Carolina Press, 1997); William Gienapp, *The Origins of the Republican Party, 1852–1856* (New York: Oxford University Press, 1987); Michael F. Holt, *The Rise and Fall of the American Whig Party: Jacksonian Politics and the Onset of the Civil War* (New York: Henry Holt, 1999), 1203.

8. Abzug, *Cosmos Crumbling*, 11–56; David Brion Davis, *Slavery and Human Progress* (New York: Oxford University Press, 1984), 107–53, 231–59.

9. Ernest Sandeen, *The Roots of Fundamentalism: British and American Millenarianism, 1800–1930* (Chicago: University of Chicago Press, 1970), 103–269. Bruce David Forbes and Jeanne Halgren Kilde, eds., *Rapture, Revelation, and the End Times: Exploring the "Left Behind" Series* (New York: Palgrave Macmillan, 2004) documents and analyzes the pervasive influence of premillennialism in contemporary religious culture.

10. Abzug, *Cosmos Crumbling*, 31–33.

11. Sandeen, *Roots of Fundamentalism*, 233–69; John McArthur, *Hard to Believe: The High Cost and Infinite Value of Following Jesus* (Chicago: Moody Press, 2002) is representative of a large number of contemporary titles by fundamentalist ministers and social activists stressing these themes. See generally the published writings of James Dobson, Pat Robertson, and Gary Bauer for other examples.

12. Stephanie McCurry, *Masters of Small Worlds: Yeoman Households, Gender Relations and the Political Culture of the Antebellum South Carolina Low Country* (New York: Oxford University Press, 1995); Christine Leigh Heyrman, *Southern Cross: The Beginnings of the Bible Belt* (New York: A. A. Knopf, 1997), 117–261.

13. For abolitionism's spiritual and intellectual opposition to institutional authority, consult Lewis Perry, *Radical Abolitionism: Anarchy and the Government of God in Antislavery Thought* (Ithaca: Cornell University Press, 1973). For a sense of the obvious contrasts to be drawn between the political circumstances of evangelical activists today and those of the abolitionist movement, see James Brewer Stewart, "The Emergence of Racial Modernity and the Rise of the White North, 1790–1840," *Journal of the Early Republic* 18 (Summer 1998): 181–217, 233–36.

14. Richard J. Carwardine, *Evangelicals and Politics in Antebellum America* (Knoxville: University of Tennessee Press, 1997); Daniel Walker Howe, *The Political Culture of the American Whigs* (Chicago: University of Chicago Press, 1979); id., "The Evangelical Movement and Political Culture in the North during the Second Party System," *Journal of American History* 77 (Mar. 1991): 1216–39.

15. Model portraits of this Whig persuasion are developed in Hugh Davis, *Leonard Bacon: New England Reformer and Antislavery Moderate* (Baton Rouge: Louisiana State University Press, 1998), and in William C. McLoughlin, *The Meaning of Henry Ward Beecher: An Essay on the Shifting Values of Mid-Victorian America* (New York: Knopf, 1970). See also George M. Marsden, *The Evangelical Mind and the New School Presbyterian Experience: A Case Study of Thought and Theology in Nineteenth-Century America* (New Haven: Yale University Press, 1970), and Howe, *Political Culture*, 1–42, 69–122.

16. Henry Brewster Stanton to James G. Birney, Mar. 21, 1839, in *The Letters of James Gillespie Birney, 1831–1857*, ed. Dwight L. Dumond, 2 vols. (New York: Henry Holt, 1938), 1:531–32.

17. *Liberator*, September 7, 1837.

18. For a broad overview of these developments, see James Brewer Stewart, *Holy Warriors: The Abolitionists and American Slavery* (New York: Hill and Wang, 1996), 75–96.

19. John Stauffer, *Black Hearts of Men: The Radical Abolitionists and the Transformation of Race* (Cambridge: Harvard University Press, 2002), 15–16, 69–70, 96–97.

20. Quotation from Holt, *Political Crisis of the 1850s*, 30. See also William J. Cooper, Jr., *The South and the Politics of Slavery, 1828–1856* (Baton Rouge: Louisana State University Press, 1978).

21. Alan Kraut, "Partisanship and Principles: The Liberty Party in Antebellum Political Culture" in *Crusaders and Compromisers*, ed. Kraut, 71–100; Louis S. Gerteis, *Morality and Utility in Antislavery Reform* (Chapel Hill: University of North Carolina Press, 1987), 86–129; James Brewer Stewart, *Joshua R. Giddings and the Tactics of Radical Politics* (Cleveland: Press of Case Western Reserve University, 1970), 84–122; Stephen E. Maizlish, *The Triumph of Sectionalism: The Transformation of Ohio Politics, 1844–1856* (Kent: Kent State University Press, 1983); Joseph G. Rayback, *Free Soil: The Election of 1848* (Lexington: University of Kentucky Press, 1970), 201–59; Reinhard Johnson, "The Liberty Party, 1840–1848: Antislavery Third Party Politics in the United States" (manuscript), chaps. 2–6; Frederick J. Blue, *The Free Soilers: Third Party Politics, 1848–1854* (Urbana: University of Illinois Press, 1973); Stanley Elkins, *Slavery: A Problem in American Institutional and Intellectual Life*, 2d ed. (Chicago: University of Chicago Press, 1968), 185–89.

22. This paragraph and the one preceding it are developed from Whitney Cross, *The Burned-Over District: A Social and Intellectual History of Enthusiastic Religion in Western New York* (Ithaca: Cornell University Press, 1950); John L. Brooke, *The Heart of the Commonwealth: Social and Political Culture in Worcester, Massachusetts, 1713–1861* (New York: Oxford University Press, 1989); Ronald P. Formisano, *The Transformation of Political Culture: Massachusetts Parties, 1790s–1840s* (New York: Oxford University, 1983); Johnson, *A Shopkeeper's Millennium*; John W. Quist, *Restless Visionaries: The Social Roots of Antebellum Reform in Alabama and Michigan* (Baton Rouge: Louisiana State University Press, 1998); David M. Ludlum, *Social Ferment in Vermont, 1791–1850* (New York: Columbia University Press, 1939); Randolph A. Roth, *The Democratic Dilemma: Religion, Reform and the Social Order in the Connecticut River Valley of Vermont, 1791–1850* (New York: Cambridge University Press, 1987); Patrick Riddleberger, *George Washington Julian: A Study in Nineteenth-Century Politics and Reform* (Indianapolis: Indiana State Historical Society Press, 1966), 1–45; Donald Martin Bluestone, "Steamboats, Sewing Machines and Bibles: The Roots of Antislavery in Illinois and the Old Northwest" (Ph.D. diss., University of Wisconsin, Madison, 1973); Stewart, *Joshua R. Giddings*.

23. One develops a clear sense of these political dynamics by reading widely in local antislavery newspapers, in a variety of regional and local studies of abolitionism, and in biographies of individual abolitionists. Titles cited in the preceding footnote are all pertinent in this respect. In addition, valuable and representative works include Douglas M. Strong, *Perfectionist Politics: Abolitionism and the Religious Tensions of American Democracy* (Syracuse: Syracuse University Press, 1999); Deborah Bingham Van Broekhoven, *The Devotion of These Women: Rhode Island in the Antislavery Network* (Amherst: University of Massachusetts Press, 2002); Nancy Hewitt, *Women's Activism and Social Change: Rochester, New York, 1822–1872* (Ithaca: Cornell University Press, 1984); Stacey M. Robertson, *Parker Pillsbury: Radical Abolitionist, Male Feminist* (Ithaca: Cornell University Press, 2000), esp. 63–91; Stewart, *Joshua R. Giddings*; Milton Sernett, *North Star Country: Upstate New York and the Crusade for African American Freedom*

(Syracuse: Syracuse University Press, 2002); Bertram Wyatt-Brown, *Lewis Tappan and the Evangelical War Against Slavery* (Cleveland: Press of Case Western Reserve University, 1969), 269–327. Using Massachusetts as his case study, Bruce Laurie, *Beyond Garrison: Antislavery and Social Reform* (Cambridge: Cambridge University Press, 2005), superbly demonstrates the sustained and significant impact of abolitionism on local and state politics.

24. For a general overview of these trends and tendencies, consult Stewart, *Holy Warriors,* chaps. 5, 6, and their accompanying bibliography. For specifics, see Jane H. Pease and William H. Pease, *They Who Would Be Free: Blacks' Search for Freedom, 1830–1861* (New York: Atheneum, 1974), 173–205.

25. These electoral tactics are particularly well discussed in Sewell, *Ballots for Freedom,* 80–201. Quotation from Wendell Phillips to Elizabeth Pease, October [n/d] 1844, Antislavery Collection, Boston Public Library.

26. William Seward to Edward A. Stanbury, Sept. 2, 1844, quoted in Glyndon Van Deusen, *William Henry Seward* (New York: Oxford University Press, 1967), 103.

27. James A. Briggs to Oran Follett, July 26, 1843, Oran Follett Papers, Cincinnati Historical Society, Cincinnati.

28. Holt, *Political Crisis of the 1850s, 63.*

29. Jonathan H. Earle, *Jacksonian Antislavery and the Politics of Free Soil, 1824–1854* (Chapel Hill; University of North Carolina Press, 2004), 169–80.

30. Gienapp, *Origins of the Republican Party,* 1–67; Holt, *Political Crisis of the 1850s,* 101–38.

31. Holt, *Political Crisis of the 1850s,* 101–38; id., *Rise and Fall of the American Whig Party,* 553–801.

32. David Brion Davis, *The Slave Power Conspiracy and the Paranoid Style* (Baton Rouge: Louisiana State University Press, 1969); Leonard L. Richards, *The Slave Power: The Free North and Southern Domination, 1780–1860* (Baton Rouge: Louisiana State University Press, 2000). Carwardine, *Evangelicals and Politics,* 199–234, gives a rich account of northern evangelicals' political alienation in the early 1850s.

33. Quoted from Michael F. Holt, *The Fate of Their Country: Politicians, Slavery Extension and the Coming of the Civil War* (New York: Oxford University Press, 2004), 91. For an overview of resistance and compliance to the Fugitive Slave Law, see Stanley W. Campbell, *The Slave Catchers: Enforcement of the Fugitive Slave Law, 1850–1860* (New York: W. W. Norton, 1970). For the selection of "fellow traveler" senators, see Gerteis, *Morality and Utility,* 99–105, 112–13, 121–24, 126–27.

34. Bailey quoted in Carwardine, *Evangelicals and Politics,* 253. Differing perspectives on the Know-Nothing Party are found in Gienapp, *Origins of the Republican Party,* Holt, *Rise and Fall of the American Whig Party,* and Foner, *Free Soil, Free Labor, Free Men.* On secular and Democratic Party contributions to antislavery, see Earle, *Jacksonian Antislavery.* For direct abolitionist attacks on slavery, see Stanley Harrold, *Subversives: Antislavery Community in Washington, D.C., 1828–1865* (Baton Rouge: Louisiana State University Press, 2003). The literature on female activism and politics can be approached through Lori Ginzberg, *Women and the Work of Benevolence: Morality, Politics and Class in the Nineteenth-Century United States* (New Haven: Yale University Press, 1990); Nancy Isenberg, *Sex and Citizenship in Antebellum America* (Chapel Hill: University of North

118   God, Garrison, and the Civil War

Carolina Press, 1998); Susan Zaeske, *Signatures of Citizenship: Petitioning, Antislavery, and Women's Political Identity* (Chapel Hill: University of North Carolina Press, 2003); and Michael D. Pierson, *Free Hearts and Free Homes: Gender and American Antislavery Politics* (Chapel Hill: University of North Carolina Press, 2003). Mary Kelley, *"Learning to Stand and Speak": Women, Education, and Public Life in America's Republic* (Chapel Hill: University of North Carolina Press, 2006), offers the most comprehensive explanation to date for the widespread emergence of women into antebellum public life.

35. Sewell, *Ballots for Freedom*, 321–42.

36. Quotation from *Liberator*, July 11, 1856; Stauffer, *Black Hearts of Men*; Jeffrey Rossbach, *Ambivalent Conspirators: John Brown, The Secret Six, and a Theory of Slave Violence* (Philadelphia: University of Pennsylvania Press, 1982); Pease and Pease, *They Who Would Be Free*, 206–77.

37. Garrison quoted in Stewart, *William Lloyd Garrison*, 165–66.

38. Wendell Phillips, *Speeches, Lectures and Letters*, 1st series (Boston: Higginson and Lee, 1863), 137–38.

39. *Liberator*, January 1, 1831.

6

Garrison at Two Hundred: The Family,
the Legacy, and the Question of Garrison's
Relevance in Contemporary America

LLOYD McKIM GARRISON

In chapter 1 of this book, David Blight poses the question, "Is the United States of the early twenty-first century truly a safe place for William Lloyd Garrison and many of his ideas?" As a direct descendant of William Lloyd Garrison, I and many in my extended family were preoccupied by that question when we gathered in August 2005 for a bicentennial celebration of our ancestor's birth. In fact, it was this celebratory event that led to the publication of this book.

During that three-day weekend reunion in and around Boston, we realized that the historian Harriet Alonso's revealing account of how Garrison raised his children in the spirit of moral reform had trickled down through succeeding generations, moving Garrison's legacy directly into the present day.[1] To be sure, Garrison's unflinching commitment to the abolitionist cause has not required us to flee from lynch mobs or endure the scorn of powerful segments of American society. It has, however, led a number of us to embrace in our own fashion the ideals of social justice to which the original "liberator" devoted his lifetime.

At first, the idea behind the gathering of William Lloyd Garrison descendants was simply to honor the bicentennial of his birth and bring together as many of his kin as possible. All were descended from the five surviving children of

William Lloyd and Helen Benson, the daughter of a Connecticut abolitionist. Two offspring died in childhood.

But a subtext emerged as 170 contemporary Garrisons arrived for the three-day celebration at the Newton Marriott Hotel outside Boston. It appeared that many had also come in search of evidence that the underlying principles that sustained Garrison's passion had endured the test of time. As Blight put it in his keynote address to the assembled family, how should we remember Garrison, and how does he speak to us today?

Daphne Harwood, one of the organizers of the reunion, remarked that until she heard Blight as well as Lois Brown and Harriet Alonso, she feared she might be suffering from an overly simplistic view of her ancestor's place in history. "It took my breath away," she said, "to hear thinking people outside the family talk of Garrison as one of the greatest Americans."

For her, as for many of us, Blight's probing question, "Is the United States [today] a safe place for William Lloyd Garrison and many of his ideas?" was very much on our minds throughout the bicentennial. Indeed, there was a sense of Garrison being brought alive not only during our deliberations in Newton, but at the two major exhibits on Garrison's life and times that opened that weekend at the Museum of African American History and the Boston Public Library. It was reassuring to know that at least on his home turf, Garrison had not been forgotten. While these two powerful displays did not address Blight's question, they left little doubt about how and why he became such a pivotal figure in American history.

That the reunion took place at all and attracted so many, including the press, was something of a miracle. There was nothing particularly well organized about the small band of Garrison descendants who journeyed to Cohasset, Massachusetts, for the reunion's first planning session in the fall of 2001. Many of us had never met. It was a blustery, cold November day, and everyone clustered around the fireplace in the home of Nan Garrison, who came straight to the point: Did anybody think a reunion was possible?

The answer was yes, and twelve participants with widely divergent backgrounds emerged as the planning committee. In addition to Nan, a historian, the group included David Garrison, a Senior Fellow at the Brookings Institution in Washington; his brother Frank, a contractor and restorer of old homes in Gloucester, Massachusetts; Daphne Harwood, a textile artist and schoolteacher residing in Vancouver, B.C.; Ethan Petitt, a graphics designer from Brooklyn, N.Y.; Edith Garrison Griffin, a Reiki practitioner living in Groton, Massachusetts; Susan and Sloan Auchincloss, publicists from Harrisburg, Pennsylvania; Arnold Garrison, a retired accountant living in Waban, Massachusetts; Tim Garrison, a computer professional in Natick, Massachusetts;

and myself, a retired journalist, and my wife, Sarah, a specialist in learning disabilities, now residing in Norfolk, Connecticut.

The Cohasset meeting was my introduction to Nan Garrison, a gracious and hugely energetic woman in her seventies. Late in life she earned her doctorate in women's history, taught at Curry College, and published *With Courage and Delicacy,* a book detailing the lives of Georgeana Woolsey, Katherine Wormely, and Elizabeth Howland, who served as nurses in the Civil War. Their treatment of the wounded during the brutal Peninsula Campaign unwittingly broke down stereotypical views of women's passive place in society, a passivity long opposed by William Lloyd Garrison, as amply noted in Brown's chapter.

Nan was not a Garrison descendant, but her interest in him long predated her marriage to the late Frederick Garrison, who came from the George Thompson branch of the family. "For as long as I can remember," she said, "certainly well before I married Fred at twenty-two, I was intellectually riveted by the courage, compassion and effectiveness of Garrison's message. He was a pacifist, but much like Jesus as he marched into the temple and cast out the money changers, he had the courage to publicly burn the Constitution for its tolerance of slavery. I couldn't let his bicentennial go by without acknowledging him with as many of his descendants as we could bring together."

The organizing group split up such tasks as canvasing descendants, compiling a database, researching a family tree, selecting a meeting place, raising money, designing a Web site, and recruiting speakers. By consensus, David Garrison became the group's chairman. Garrisonian frugality was the rule. Members took turns hosting meetings in their homes. Much like William Lloyd Garrison's American Anti-Slavery Society during the 1840s and 1850s, the organizing group had minimal administration and no overhead to speak of. Perhaps mindful of William Lloyd's celebrated serenity, the group's discourse was civil, and disagreements seldom lasted for long. As planning went forward, Frank Garrison observed that "one aspect of William Lloyd's persona was a profound inner calmness that I felt among all the other Garrisons working on the bicentennial. It was an unflappable quality of acceptance and anticipation that the proper goal would be achieved with time."

And in time, it was. As the reunion got under way, it struck many of us that Garrison's radicalism was very much relevant in an America where racism is still prevalent and in a nation bitterly divided over social and cultural issues at home and an increasingly unpopular war abroad. Many felt that were Garrison alive today, he would have found the contentiousness in American society all too familiar and the need for change never more pressing.

Edith Garrison Griffin found herself not a little appalled that Garrison's principles still needed to be applied in today's America. "As we listened to readings aloud of excerpts from his writings at the Museum of African American History," she recalled, "a number of us were struck by how timely William Lloyd's words are. You could publish what he wrote one hundred fifty years ago and they would be highly relevant today." For Griffin, the bicentennial revealed a few surprises about Garrison's personal qualities. One was learning about his playful sense of humor. She was also impressed by "his devotion to his family and his enjoyment of music, especially hymns sung by his family and friends in his home."

Garrison definitely had an eye on his place in history. As Alonso pointed out, he was so determined that the principles for which he stood be passed on through his offspring that he named three of his four boys after other leading abolitionists. One of them, Wendell Phillips Garrison, was my great-grandfather.

And what were those principles which Garrison sought to enshrine in children? Not just the abolition of slavery and the emancipation of women, but also a strong belief in the power of nonviolent resistance in overcoming all forms of injustice. My father, Lloyd Kirkham Garrison, was especially fond of pointing out that Garrison's espousal of passive resistance had greatly impressed Leo Tolstoy, whose writings on the subject were adapted and put into practice in India by Mahatma Gandhi, and through Gandhi came back full circle to Martin Luther King, Jr.

To what extent have any of these tenets been passed on through additional generations of Garrisons? David Garrison, the reunion's moderator, spoke authoritatively on this matter on the second night of the reunion at the Tremont Street Temple, where William Lloyd Garrison often spoke: "We Garrisons seek to carry forward as best we can the core beliefs of this great and good man. We are noisy, engaged public citizens. We serve on town committees, and even run for local office. We are active in our churches, some of us anyway. We oversee the local community centers and serve on nonprofit boards. We are writers and journalists. We join peace marches at the drop of a hat. We go to Washington and work for a president and the Congress."

David Garrison, descended from the William Lloyd Garrison Jr. branch of the family, was one of those who went to Washington. It was a route initially taken with only a dim sense that he might actually be beginning a lifetime of distinguished public service. "I must admit that as a youth," he said, "I was a lot more impressed with my Dad's exploits as a member of the 1932 and 1936 U.S. Olympic hockey teams." That changed when his father retired from his career as a sales representative for a knit goods company and became increasingly engrossed in town affairs in Lincoln, Massachusetts. "When I was in my early teens," he says, "Mom and Dad would take me to town meetings.

Later, Dad was elected a selectman and would bring home stories of the latest town controversies, all of which whetted my appetite."

When embarking on his own career, it seemed only natural that David sought to serve the public by advocating for social justice. Before joining the Brookings Institution, he worked for a dozen nonprofit organizations and public agencies, including the Office for Civil Rights at the Department of Health and Human Services in the Clinton administration, which he headed for a year. "It finally came to me that William Lloyd would have approved the course I had taken," he reflected, "even though I wasn't really conscious of following his example as I went from one public post to the next."

David Garrison's brother, Frank, also credits his father's civic-mindedness as a determining influence. But he recalls two other people who were equally important role models in the Garrison mold. One was his Aunt Tita Garrison Emerson, a compassionate Quaker and untiring community activist who could be counted on to lead demonstrations and hand out leaflets supporting numerous local causes. (This was hardly coincidental; in William Lloyd's day, Quaker radicals were among his staunchest allies.) The other was his uncle, David Lloyd Garrison, who followed Garrisonian principles of nonresistance as a determined pacifist and conscientious objector during World War II. "I learned to be socially conscious by tagging along with these wonderful folks," said Frank.

Anne Layzer, another member of the William Lloyd Garrison Jr. branch of the family, recalled that "first among all other traits, this family is riddled with writers: authors, playwrights, scriptwriters, editors, newspaper and magazine reporters, writers of newsletters, theses, briefs and motions, op-ed pieces, letters to the editor, poems, hymns, and light verse." Anne also noted that family members were predominantly liberal and over the years produced only one minister, Kate Layzer, a Congregationalist.

Looking back on his Garrison forebears, Sloan Auchincloss, who comes from the Wendell Phillips branch, was impressed with how many in his family took up the cause of women's reproductive rights, the key battleground for women's rights in the modern day. Sloan, who grew up in the Boston area, recalled that "the region had a split personality when it came to personal freedom. Though liberal in character, Boston took its sexual mores from the Catholic Church, which was dominated by the powerful archbishop Richard Cardinal Cushing.

"Cushing cowed the Massachusetts General Assembly into banning birth control and the distribution of any information about its practice. That didn't stop my parents from running car shuttles to Providence, Rhode Island, so that women could get reproductive health care." Sloan's wife, Susan, is a former director of Planned Parenthood in the Susquehanna Valley of Pennsylvania, and Sloan has been an active supporter of Project Leap Forward, a program designed to give an educational boost to children in underperforming inner-city schools in the Harrisburg area. Sloan and Susan played an important role as cotreasurers of the committee organizing the reunion.

My own life has been shaped in part not only by Garrison's career as a writer and editor of the *Liberator,* but by the knowledge that his son, Wendell Phillips Garrison, became the literary editor of the *Nation.* Another journalistic influence was Henry Villard, who married Garrison's beloved daughter, Helen Frances "Fanny" Garrison. The two met during the Civil War when Villard, a celebrated *New York Tribune* war correspondent, came to call on her father.

Villard was the classic immigrant success story. He had arrived from Germany a decade before speaking no English and with only three dollars in his pocket. After the Civil War and his marriage to Fanny, he accumulated a small fortune investing in railroads and helping Thomas Edison launch General Electric. But he remained a journalist at heart and used much of his wealth to finance the *Nation* and the *New York Evening Post.* He also funded the Niagara Movement, the precursor of the National Association for the Advancement of Colored People (NAACP).

It was the Garrison–Villard connection that first moved me to become a journalist. Fully conscious of my Garrison heritage, I found myself being drawn to Africa in the early 1960s to report on the world's newest abolitionist movement — Africa's struggle to overturn white rule in the Congo, Angola, Rhodesia, and South Africa. I had just quit working in radio and television news in order to switch to print journalism. From a professional standpoint, Africa in the summer of 1960 was an ideal place for a freelance writer, as no American newspapers had correspondents based permanently anywhere south of the Sahara. My wife and I arrived in Leopoldville in the former Belgian Congo just in time for the peaceful Independence Day ceremonies in June of 1960, a year when many other African colonies also gained their freedom. But within a week, Congolese soldiers mutinied against their Belgian officers and Prime Minister Patrice Lumumba lost control of his army. The ensuing chaos led to civil war and the UN's first attempt at peacekeeping. While reporting on these events, I was mindful of the fact that the Congo once served as one of the prime staging areas for the transatlantic slave trade that so deeply incensed my great-great-grandfather.

One lasting impression I absorbed in the Congo was that African violence against the Belgians never reflected an all-embracing racist pathology. When I first encountered nervous Congolese soldiers at roadblocks on the road in from the Leopoldville airport, the guns were lowered and frowns turned to smiles once I identified myself as an American. I went on to report on other West African countries for the *New York Times,* and though I was a distinct minority on a black continent that had suffered numerous indignities at the hands of Europeans, I never experienced any racism or overt hostility merely because I was white. I spent over five years covering Africa from my base in Lagos, Nigeria, where Sarah and I could walk down any street at any hour of the day or night and never feel at risk. The same could not be said for the New York we had left behind us.

Sadly, this is no longer the case in Nigeria. Guns and crime and tribal and religious conflict were among the legacies of the Nigerian civil war in the late 1960s. The rented house that was our home in Lagos for more than five years is now surrounded by high walls topped by barbed wire.

In his quiet way, my father, Lloyd Kirkham Garrison, a lawyer, courageously lived out the family's historic principles. In 1924, when he was just starting his law practice in New York, there was a knock at his office door. Two African Americans introduced themselves and asked whether he was indeed Lloyd Garrison. When he answered yes, they asked him to be treasurer of the fledging National Urban League. He agreed. Dad went on to become its president and often took me with him to annual Urban League conventions. Like his forebear, Dad often stayed in the homes of black colleagues when he traveled with league members because so many hotels, even in the North, were segregated. Dad was also active in the NAACP, was a trustee of Howard University, and took on the defense of Arthur Miller, Langston Hughes, and J. Robert Oppenheimer during the worst of the McCarthy era. Like William Lloyd, he never thought twice about going against "the wind and the tide of popular clamor."[2]

My father had a much more intimate sense than I have of what it meant to be directly descended from William Lloyd Garrison. When Dad lost his father to typhoid at an early age, his grandfather, Wendell Phillips Garrison, helped fill the void. He often told Dad stories of what it was like growing up in the modest Garrison home in the Roxbury section of Boston, which served as a home away from home for many visiting abolitionists, black and white. A frequent guest was Frederick Douglass. As Grandpa Wendell told Dad, "You never knew when you woke up in the morning who might be sleeping in the bed next to you."

By all accounts the five Garrison children thrived in this heady environment. "Our reward was great and lasting," recalled Garrison's son Francis, speaking of the many visitors. "I wish it were in my power adequately . . . to tell of the enlivening talk, the animated discussions on moral questions, and, in hours of relaxation, the wit and merriment, which made all outside attractions pale beside those of our own home."[3]

Yet Francis also recalled that poverty was not far from the family's door. The *Liberator,* which never made money, depended on generous benefactors, some of whom split with Garrison over his stand on equal rights for women and his refusal to engage in politics. When on the road, Garrison often could not afford a hotel and relied on the hospitality of local black abolitionists. When traveling with black colleagues, he sat in the Blacks Only section of the train. African Americans were the biggest subscribers to the *Liberator,* and it was they who stood watch night and day after a gallows was erected outside his home in 1834. They often shadowed him as he moved about Boston, a city angrily split over the issue of slavery. On one occasion a mob seized Garrison and nearly lynched him. He was saved only when the mayor hustled him into a nearby jail.

For more than three decades Garrison soldiered on, fully aware that the state of South Carolina had put a five-thousand-dollar bounty on his head. Knowing that William Lloyd had brushed aside this threat made it a lot easier for me to ignore a fifty-thousand-dollar bounty the Nigerian government had put on my head in an attempt to hasten my exit from rebel Biafra at the outset of the Nigerian civil war in 1966.

Too soon after he died in 1876, Garrison's life became reduced to little more than a footnote in high school history books entirely written and produced by white scholars. As David Blight reminds us in his magisterial book *Race and Reunion,* it was African Americans who did what they could to keep his memory alive.[4] On the first centenary of Garrison's birth in 1905, most commemorative events around New England were organized and attended overwhelmingly by African Americans. At the time, blacks felt under siege by the failure of Reconstruction to guarantee the rights Garrison had fought so boldly to achieve only a few decades before. By 1905, segregation was pervasive, blacks were disenfranchised in the South, and lynchings were common.

This was the historical backdrop as the principal speaker advanced to the podium at the one-hundredth anniversary celebration in Boston's Faneuil Hall. The speaker was the noted black orator Reverend Reverdy C. Ransom. "Garrison," recalled Ransom, "was not bound to the slave by ties of race. In his struggle for freedom, there was no hope of personal gain, no voice of popular approval save that of his conscience and his God. Business interests regarded him as an influence that disturbed and injured commerce and trade; the church opposed him; the North repudiated him; the South burned him in effigy. Yet almost single-handed and alone, Garrison fought on."[5]

Well, not quite alone. This consistent embrace of Garrison and his ideals by black American activists like Ransom was one development that was impressed upon all of us in the course of the reunion and during our visits to the two exhibits on Garrison in Boston. As Blight suggested in his keynote address, one of the reasons for the extraordinary bond between Garrison and African Americans had to do with the fact that Garrison shared with many blacks of his day what it meant to be deprived of schooling beyond a few years in grade school, to be caught as a youngster in poverty's vice and still manage to escape by a combination of good luck and extraordinary perseverance.

The Saturday evening gala at the Tremont Temple, sponsored by the Museum of African American History, underscored this point. Open to the general public and well attended, there were few white faces besides those of us Garrisons in that swinging, foot-stomping audience. As it had done so many times in the past, Boston's black community had once again assembled to commemorate Garrison's legacy.

Not since Martin Luther King Jr. ignited the civil rights movement of the 1960s have we seen anyone like William Lloyd Garrison emerging to lead the cause of a more just and nonviolent America. This might be partly due to the fact that these are not times that welcome calls for radical change. While William Lloyd might have espoused his ideals today without receiving death threats, his pacifism and burning of the Constitution would be seen by many as blatantly unpatriotic and evidence of disloyalty to his country.

Our bicentennial celebration attempted to cast a bright light on the nature of this unusual man, and for a moment succeeded in drawing considerable attention to his accomplishments. In a notable reflection on the bicentennial, the *Boston Globe* columnist Adrian Walker observed, "As Blight so powerfully pointed out, much of the history of the Civil War has become sanitized. That's been unfortunate for Garrison, who can't be appreciated at all without understanding his courage and outsized passion. For a while over the weekend, some of that history came blazing back to life in a way that a Freedom Trail can barely suggest."[6]

But if the level of popular demand on Amazon.com for information about Garrison is any indication, the "blaze" Walker referred to has all but flickered out. One year after the bicentennial, Amazon.com had on hand more than fifty new and used copies of Henry Mayer's critically acclaimed Garrison biography, *All on Fire*, which was nominated for the National Book Award. The price had slipped to a lowly seventy-five cents.

So how should we remember Garrison in the context of today's ongoing struggle by blacks in America to achieve full equality? Mayer had one answer, which was yes, Garrison will always be remembered for igniting the successful movement to end slavery, yet he left us with something more powerful and yet so fragile: "the vision of a nation that might some day transcend the phobia of color and the barriers of race."[7]

While that "courage and outsized passion" that Walker wrote about remains a standard for future American reformers to emulate, it will take much continuing work by historians and future Garrisons to sustain our ancestor as a living and disturbing presence in American life. As Frederick Douglass told a memorial service honoring Garrison in Washington, D.C., "It was the glory of this man that he could stand alone with the truth and calmly await the result." But as Mayer concluded, "We await it still."[8]

Notes

1. Harriet Alonso, *Growing Up Abolitionist* (Amherst: University of Massachusetts Press, 2002).

2. In the *Liberator* for 10 September 1836, William Lloyd Garrison wrote, "Every moral and religious reform . . . is struggling against the wind and the tide of popular clamor."

3. Alonso, *Growing Up Abolitionist,* 71.

4. David W. Blight, *Race and Reunion: The Civil War in American Memory* (Cambridge: Belknap Press of the Harvard University Press, 2001), 364–65.

5. *Guardian,* Boston, 14 December 1905.

6. *Boston Globe,* 8 August 2005.

7. Henry Mayer, *All on Fire* (New York: St. Martin's Press, 1998), 630.

8. Ibid., 631.

Contributors

RICHARD J. M. BLACKETT is Andrew Jackson Professor of History, Vanderbilt University.

DAVID W. BLIGHT is Class of '54 Professor of History and Director, the Gilder Lehrman Center for the Study of Slavery, Resistance and Abolition.

LOIS A. BROWN is Associate Professor of English and Director of the Weissman Center for Leadership and the Liberal Arts, Mount Holyoke College.

LLOYD MCKIM GARRISON, a retired journalist, is a great-great-grandson of William Lloyd Garrison.

BRUCE LAURIE is Professor of History Emeritus, University of Massachusetts, Amherst.

JAMES BREWER STEWART is James Wallace Professor of History, Emeritus, Macalester College.

Index

Abiel Smith School, 87–88

abolitionism: of African Americans, 46,
49–50, 54–63, 64–65, 100, 102, 105,
111; authoritarianism and, 99; children in, 60–63, 64–65; civil rights and,
7; Civil War and, xi, 8–9, 53, 94, 96–
98, 111–13; disunionism and, 6–7, 8,
94, 102; electoral politics and, xi, 7, 8,
104–7; evangelicalism compared, xi,
94–95, 98–101, 102–9, 112–13; feminism and, x–xi, 7, 21–22, 42–43, 44–
45, 47–56, 102; government and, 10;
immediatism in, 5–6, 101; memory of,
2–3; moral perfectionism and, 6; nonresistance and, 6, 25, 94, 102; pacifism
and, 6, 7–8; petitioning in, 43–44, 67;
political agency of, xi, 96–98, 99–101,
102, 104–7, 108, 110–11, 111–13;
principles of, for Garrison, 6–10, 41–
42, 102, 122; radicalism and, 6–10;
reign of terror against, 100–101, 101–
2; religion and, x, 6, 98–99; Republican Party and, 110–13; scholarship on,
96–98; terminology of, 2, 47–49, 50,
54, 55–56, 96, 99; Whig Party and,
101–9, 112–13; of whites, 47–49, 50–
54, 65–67; of women, 21–22, 24–25,
42–45, 47–56, 100, 105. *See also*
transatlantic movement

abortion, 96, 97, 100, 123–24

Adam, William, 22–23

Adams, Abigail, 43–44

Adams, John, 43

Africa, 14–15, 18, 19–20, 124–25, 126

African Americans: abolitionism of generally, 46, 49–50, 54–63, 64–65, 100,
102, 105, 111; in Boston Female Anti-
Slavery Society, 63–65; civil rights of,
vii–viii, viii–ix, 7, 51–54; colonization
and, 14–15, 16; commemoration of
Garrison by, 126–27; female, 46, 49–
50, 54–63, 64–65; journalism of, 46,
49–50, 56–58, 62–63; in Liberty
Party, 82; political agency of generally,